Copyright Page

Never Put All Your Eggs in One Basket

Copyright © 2024 by Kim Ruff Moore

Published by Ruff Moore Media

All rights reserved.

No part of this publication may be reproduced, distributed, or transmitted in any form or by any means, including photocopying, recording, or other electronic or mechanical methods, without the prior written permission of the publisher, except in the case of brief quotations embodied in critical reviews and certain other noncommercial uses permitted by copyright law.

For permissions or inquiries, visit:

www.kimruffmoore.com

www.ruffmooremedia.com

First Edition: 2024

Printed in the United States of America

ISBN: 9798300837938

To My Son Spencer—You are brilliant! I cannot wait to see what God does with you. Love you

Other Titles by Kim Ruff Moore

Children's Books:

- *Suzzie Mocha Series*
- *Kirby the Koala Series*
- *Sergio the Studio Mouse Series*
- *Spence Seven Series*
- *Harper Sharper Series*
- *Pavo the Parrot*
- *Otis the Brave Brown Bear*
- *Rosie and the Easter Egg Hunt*
- *The Land of Unicorns Series*
- *Bria Gets New Braids For School*
- *Elo the Elephant Forgets Everything*
- *Piper the Pretty Pink Dinosaur Series*
- *Kids Prayers*
- *Mommy, I Can Do It Series*
- *You Are Humongous*

- *I Want to Sing Like Whitney*
- *A Very Purple Day*
- *Oliver and the Ocean*
- *I Believe Who God Says I Am*
- *Pebo Pig Prefers Pancakes with Ketchup*
- *Sanford the Sloth*

Adult Books:

- *Marriage Releases*
- *God's Favor, Serendipity*
- *Cuffed*
- *Waymaker*
- *Girl Mash the Gas: Stop Procrastinating*
- *Girl Forgive Them and Move On*
- *Secrets of a Successful Publisher*
- *Write Children's Books*

Table of Contents

Introduction

Something Has To Change

The Warren Buffett Mindset

Earvin "Magic" Johnson

Mary Kay Ash

Cathy Hughes

Sheila Johnson

Celebrities Who Get It

Spread Your Eggs

Five Americans Who Got It

Talented And Creative People

Peace Of Mind

Parable Of The Talents

You Can Do It

Bibliography - Sources Cited

Introduction

The stories of business moguls like Warren Buffet, Mary Kay Ash and Magic Johnson fascinated me. All of them have a diversified financial portfolio. They inspired me to want more in life. I was unsure how to do it, but the desire was created. Their unparalleled business acumen and the ability to diversify, creating a myriad of revenue streams, inspired me to envision a life beyond the constraints of financial instability. As someone who had long lived paycheck to paycheck, the realization struck hard – I needed to chart a different course if I ever wanted to break free from the cycle of financial uncertainty. This is the story of my journey, a quest for financial independence and a determination to carve out a path that leads to prosperity.

The realization of changing my life hit me like a lightning bolt during a particularly challenging month. I had just paid my car note, utilities, and other necessities, leaving me with a paltry amount that vanished before I could even catch a breath. The fragility of relying on a single income source became glaringly apparent, and I knew I needed to make a change.

With a background in music, I decided to tap into my passion for songwriting and singing. I began performing at local venues, uploading my music online, and exploring avenues for royalties. It wasn't long before my songs gained traction, and I started receiving royalty checks – a modest stream of income that didn't depend on a fixed salary.

Encouraged by this initial success, I delved into entrepreneurship. I founded several small companies, each catering to a different niche. From selling physical music CD's to providing consulting services, I diversified my business ventures. Not every endeavor turned into a gold mine, but the cumulative effect began to make a noticeable difference in my financial landscape.

As my entrepreneurial spirit soared, I ventured into the world of intellectual property. I realized the potential of licensing my creations – from music to innovative business ideas. This approach not only added another income stream but also secured my work's long-term value.

The decision to write books wasn't just about sharing my experiences; it became another avenue for generating income. My first book chronicled my journey, offering practical advice on relationships. The success of that book opened doors to additional writing opportunities, creating a passive income stream through book royalties.

In the symphony of life, I found my unique melody by harmonizing various talents and passions. As a professional singer, motivational speaker, and songwriter, I navigated the diverse realms of creativity, aiming not only to entertain but to inspire and uplift. Determined to explore the vast landscape of opportunities, I ventured into the world of publishing songs, crafting meaningful lyrics that resonated with the hearts of many. Recognizing the power of words beyond melodies, I delved into the art of writing books, weaving narratives that carried the essence of my experiences and lessons learned. Embracing the visual language of creativity, I harnessed the skill of graphic design to give life to my artistic vision. In a world often urging specialization, I chose a path less traveled—deciding not to confine my aspirations to a single basket. This is the story of how I orchestrated a symphony of talents to not just monetize but to create a myriad of options, refusing to limit the boundless potential that exists within the spectrum of my capabilities.

The journey unfolded with each note sung, each word written, and every graphic design meticulously crafted. My decision to diversify wasn't just about financial gain; it was a conscious choice to lead a life rich in experiences and possibilities. As a professional singer, I poured my soul into performances, understanding the transformative power of music to evoke emotions and provoke thought. Simultaneously, my venture into motivational speaking became a platform to share not just melodies but the stories behind them—lessons learned, challenges overcome, and dreams pursued.

Publishing songs was an empowering step, allowing me to reach a broader audience and connect with people on a profound level. The lyrics became anthems for those navigating the intricate dance of life, resonating with the highs and lows we all encounter. The decision to pen down my thoughts into books was a natural progression, an avenue to delve deeper into the nuances of human experience and provide a lasting legacy beyond the ephemeral nature of a song.

With graphic design, I discovered a visual language that complimented my auditory and literary expressions. Each design became a canvas to communicate ideas, emotions, and concepts, expanding the scope of my artistic endeavors. In a world where specialization often dominates, I embraced the challenge of wearing multiple hats, thriving on the dynamic interplay between different forms of creativity.

The decision not to put all my eggs in one basket wasn't merely a financial strategy; it was a commitment to a life of perpetual growth and exploration. By diversifying my pursuits, I created many possibilities that transcended the conventional boundaries of a single career. This is the narrative of how I transformed my passions into a symphony, a multifaceted approach to life that continues to evolve with each new note, word, and design.

The journey of diversification wasn't without its hurdles and uncertainties. Balancing the demands of singing, speaking, writing, and designing required a delicate choreography of time management and relentless dedication. Yet, it was precisely in this dynamic dance that I discovered the resilience within me.

Monetizing my passions became a strategic endeavor, turning each skill into a revenue stream that not only sustained my livelihood but also funded new ventures. The songs I sang and wrote not only resonated with audiences but also found their place in commercials, films, and events. Motivational speaking engagements transformed into workshops, empowering others to navigate their paths with resilience and determination.

Publishing my songs and books not only provided artistic satisfaction but also created a legacy that transcended the ephemeral nature of live performances. The graphic designs, initially a complement to my other pursuits, took on a life of their own. From album covers to promotional materials, each design became a visual representation of my artistic brand, attracting diverse opportunities in the expansive world of multimedia.

The decision to diversify was, at its core, a decision to be the orchestrator of my own destiny. It allowed me to navigate the unpredictable twists of the creative industry, ensuring that my passion for expression wasn't confined to the limitations of a single avenue. As I continued to explore the synergies between my various talents, I found that each skill enhanced the other, creating a holistic and enriching artistic experience.

Ultimately, this narrative isn't just about monetization—it's about embracing the multidimensional nature of creativity. It's a testament to the belief that by refusing to limit myself to a singular path, I opened doors to a multitude of opportunities and possibilities. This is the story of how I transformed my passions into not just a career but a kaleidoscopic journey that continues to unfold with every endeavor.

Real estate became the cornerstone of my financial strategy. Setting a goal of Investing in properties allowed me to map out a plan to build equity and generate rental income. The real estate market's appreciation over time further bolstered my financial portfolio, providing a stable foundation amidst economic uncertainties.

Reflecting on my journey, I realized that so many Americans were trapped in the same paycheck-to-paycheck cycle. It fueled my determination to share my story, hoping it would inspire others to break free from financial constraints. My book aims to be a guide, offering practical steps and insights into creating diverse income streams, tailored to individual talents and passions.

As I write the final chapters of my book, I can't help but feel a sense of accomplishment. From the struggles of living paycheck to paycheck, I've emerged with a portfolio of income streams that safeguard me against financial instability. My story is not just about my success; it's an invitation for others to rewrite their financial narratives, one diversified income stream at a time. Embarking on the journey of transforming my life from one of financial scarcity to abundance has been a profound and empowering experience. As I reflect on the twists and turns of my personal and professional life, I find myself compelled to share the insights, strategies, and lessons that have paved the way for this remarkable transformation. This book is a testament to the belief that anyone can shift their financial trajectory by cultivating multiple streams of income.

In these pages, I will chronicle my ventures into entrepreneurship, sharing the challenges and victories that came with creating and managing successful companies. The exploration of my passion for music, from songwriting to pursuing a career in professional singing, will serve as a testament to the notion that one can turn their hobbies into lucrative sources of income. Additionally, the evolution of my journey into the realm of public speaking, writing books, and venturing into real estate will be laid bare, offering readers a roadmap for diversifying their own income streams.

My decision to pen this narrative stems from a desire to inspire others who may find themselves in the throes of financial limitation. By sharing my experiences and the strategies that propelled me from lack to plenty, I hope to empower individuals to pursue their dreams with unwavering determination. Through the highs and lows, this book will serve as a guide, offering practical advice and motivational anecdotes for those who aspire to break free from financial constraints and manifest a life of abundance through various avenues.

Join me on this expedition through the pages of my life, where resilience, innovation, and a relentless pursuit of success converge to redefine what's possible. May this chronicle serve as both a source of inspiration and a practical roadmap for those ready to embark on their own transformative journey towards financial prosperity and fulfillment. It is my sincere prayer that this book will bless you and change your life forever. I took a long look at my life and assessed my gift and talents to see how best to monetize and increase my net worth and options.

Something Has to Change

In the era of instant gratification and societal expectations, it's disheartening to witness how our values have shifted towards materialism and conspicuous consumption. The relentless pursuit of name brands, flashy cars, and sprawling mansions seems to have overshadowed the importance of genuine experiences and meaningful connections.

We've become a society fixated on external appearances, investing heavily in plastic surgery, perfectly manicured nails, meticulously styled hair, and layers of makeup. The pressure to conform to societal beauty standards has reached unprecedented levels, leaving many trapped in a cycle of superficial enhancements that often come at a hefty price.

Our penchant for indulgence extends beyond personal appearances to our leisure activities. Whether it's lavish vacations, excessive dining out, or the constant craving for fast food, our obsession with instant pleasure has put a considerable strain on our finances. The allure of entertainment and sports further contributes to this culture of excess, pushing us to spend beyond our means in the pursuit of temporary joy.

The ubiquitous presence of alcohol as a social lubricant has also become a staple in our quest for escape. While the occasional indulgence may appear harmless, the frequency with which we turn to alcohol to cope with the stresses of daily life is concerning. I personally do not drink. Excessive alcohol consumption not only drains our financial resources but also has broader implications for our physical and mental well-being.

In the midst of this consumerist frenzy, the art of saving and financial planning often takes a backseat. The accumulation of debt becomes a constant companion as we chase after the next trend or desirable experience. The vicious cycle of overspending leads to financial woes, creating a ripple effect that can impact not only our present but also our future.

It's crucial to reflect on the values that underpin our choices and question whether the pursuit of material possessions and fleeting pleasures truly brings lasting happiness. Shifting our focus towards more sustainable and fulfilling endeavors, fostering genuine connections, and prioritizing financial prudence can pave the way for a more balanced and fulfilling life. Breaking free from the shackles of materialism requires a conscious effort to redefine our priorities and resist the societal pressures that often lead us astray.

Amidst the barrage of societal expectations, it's imperative to recognize that the pursuit of genuine happiness lies in experiences that go beyond the superficial. Rather than seeking validation through material possessions, we should channel our energy towards building meaningful relationships, fostering personal growth, and contributing to our communities.

The constant bombardment of advertisements and societal norms can make it challenging to resist the allure of consumerism. However, embracing a more minimalist and intentional lifestyle can serve as a counterbalance to the culture of excess. This involves decluttering not just our physical spaces but also our minds, allowing room for experiences that enrich our lives in ways money cannot measure.

While there's nothing inherently wrong with enjoying the occasional luxury or treating ourselves to life's pleasures, it's essential to approach such indulgences with mindfulness and moderation. Budgeting and financial planning become invaluable tools in regaining control over our spending habits and steering clear of the pitfalls of debt.

Investing time and resources in experiences that contribute to personal growth and well-being can be a powerful antidote to the emptiness often associated with material pursuits. Pursuing hobbies, learning new skills, and engaging in activities that align with our passions can provide a deeper sense of fulfillment and purpose.

Moreover, reevaluating societal standards of beauty and success can help break free from the cycle of unnecessary cosmetic enhancements. Embracing individuality and challenging conventional norms can contribute to a more inclusive and accepting society, where self-worth is not dictated by external appearances.

In the realm of leisure and entertainment, finding joy in simple pleasures and cultivating a sense of gratitude for what we have can lead to a more content and financially stable life. Rather than constantly chasing the next thrill, appreciating the present moment and the people around us can foster a lasting sense of happiness.

Ultimately, steering away from the societal tide of materialism requires a conscious effort to redefine our values and prioritize what truly matters. By cultivating a sense of mindfulness, embracing a more intentional lifestyle, and making informed financial decisions, we can pave the way for a society that values genuine connections, personal fulfillment, and long-term financial well-being.

In contemplating the societal shift away from materialism and embracing financial wisdom, one can find guidance and inspiration in various Christian scriptures and analogies that emphasize responsible stewardship and a focus on enduring values.

Matthew 6:19-21 (NIV):

"Do not store up for yourselves treasures on earth, where moths and vermin destroy, and where thieves break in and steal. But store up for yourselves treasures in heaven, where moths and vermin do not destroy, and where thieves do not break in and steal. For where your treasure is, there your heart will be also."

This passage reminds us of the impermanence of material possessions and encourages a shift in focus towards eternal values. Investing in relationships, personal growth, and the well-being of others aligns with the idea of storing treasures in heaven.

Proverbs 21:20 (NIV):

"The wise store up choice food and olive oil, but fools gulp theirs down."

This Proverb emphasizes the importance of prudence and foresight in managing resources. Being financially wise involves thoughtful planning and the avoidance of impulsive and excessive consumption.

Luke 14:28-30 (NIV):

"Suppose one of you wants to build a tower. Won't you first sit down and estimate the cost to see if you have enough money to complete it? For if you lay the foundation and are not able to finish it, everyone who sees it will ridicule you, saying, 'This person began to build and wasn't able to finish.'"

This analogy underscores the significance of financial planning and the consequences of not considering the long-term implications of our decisions. Just as one would plan before building a tower, being financially responsible involves careful consideration of our financial foundations.

Matthew 25:14-30 (NIV) - The Parable of the Bags of Gold:

This parable emphasizes the importance of stewardship and using our resources wisely. The servants who invested and multiplied their talents were commended, while the one who buried his talent faced consequences. It serves as a reminder of the responsibility we have in using our financial resources for good.

1 Timothy 6:17-19 (NIV):

"Command those who are rich in this present world not to be arrogant nor to put their hope in wealth, which is so uncertain, but to put their hope in God, who richly provides us with everything for our enjoyment. Command them to do good, to be rich in good deeds, and to be generous and willing to share. In this way, they will lay up treasure for themselves as a firm foundation for the coming age, so that they may take hold of the life that is truly life."

This passage encourages a perspective shift from reliance on material wealth to a focus on doing good, being generous, and building a firm foundation in faith. It aligns with the idea that true life and fulfillment come from spiritual richness and **Philippians 4:11-13 (NIV):**
"I am not saying this because I am in need, for I have learned to be content whatever the circumstances. I know

what it is to be in need, and I know what it is to have plenty. I have learned the secret of being content in any and every situation, whether well fed or hungry, whether living in plenty or in want. I can do all this through him who gives me strength."

This passage from Philippians underscores the virtue of contentment, emphasizing that true strength and contentment come from a reliance on God rather than material possessions. By cultivating contentment, we can resist the constant urge to accumulate more and find fulfillment in the present moment.

Luke 16:10 (NIV):

"Whoever can be trusted with very little can also be trusted with much, and whoever is dishonest with very little will also be dishonest with much."

This verse speaks to the principle of faithful stewardship. By being responsible with the resources, opportunities, and wealth entrusted to us, we demonstrate integrity and faithfulness. This aligns with the idea that how we handle smaller financial matters reflects our readiness for greater responsibilities.

Proverbs 3:9-10 (NIV):

"Honor the Lord with your wealth, with the firstfruits of all your crops; then your barns will be filled to overflowing, and your vats will brim over with new wine."

This Proverb encourages a spirit of generosity and the practice of giving back. By prioritizing offerings and charitable acts with our financial blessings, we honor God and contribute to the well-being of others, fostering a sense of abundance in our own lives.

Ecclesiastes 5:10 (NIV):

"Whoever loves money never has enough; whoever loves wealth is never satisfied with their income. This too is meaningless."

This verse from Ecclesiastes warns against the pursuit of wealth for its own sake. It highlights the futility of an insatiable desire for more and emphasizes the importance of finding contentment beyond material accumulation.

James 1:17 (NIV):

"Every good and perfect gift is from above, coming down from the Father of the heavenly lights, who does not change like shifting shadows."

Recognizing that all we have is ultimately a gift from God encourages an attitude of gratitude. Understanding that material possessions are temporary and that our ultimate source of security is in God can shape our perspective on financial decisions and priorities.

In summary, integrating these biblical principles into our approach to finances encourages a holistic view that includes contentment, responsible stewardship, generosity, and reliance on God. By aligning our financial choices with these values, we can navigate the challenges of a materialistic society with wisdom and faith, fostering a sense of fulfillment that goes beyond fleeting material possessions.

Matthew 6:24 (NIV):

"No one can serve two masters. Either you will hate the one

and love the other, or you will be devoted to the one and despise the other. You cannot serve both God and money." This verse serves as a stark reminder of the incompatibility of serving both God and the pursuit of wealth. It emphasizes the need to prioritize our devotion to God over the relentless pursuit of material gain, highlighting the spiritual consequences of an overly materialistic mindset.

Proverbs 30:8-9 (NIV):

"Keep falsehood and lies far from me; give me neither poverty nor riches, but give me only my daily bread. Otherwise, I may have too much and disown you and say, 'Who is the Lord?'

Or I may become poor and steal, and so dishonor the name of my God."

This prayerful passage from Proverbs reflects a plea for moderation and contentment. It acknowledges the potential pitfalls of extreme wealth or poverty, recognizing that both can lead to spiritual challenges. The request for "daily bread" signifies a desire for sufficiency rather than excess.

Hebrews 13:5 (NIV):

"Keep your lives free from the love of money and be content with what you have, because God has said, 'Never will I leave you; never will I forsake you.'"

This verse combines the call for contentment with a reassurance of God's constant presence. It encourages believers to find contentment in God's faithfulness rather than the pursuit of material possessions, reinforcing the idea that true security comes from a relationship with the divine.

1 Timothy 5:8 (NIV):

"Anyone who does not provide for their relatives, and especially for their own household, has denied the faith and is worse than an unbeliever."

This verse underscores the importance of financial responsibility within the context of family and community. It emphasizes the need to prioritize providing for one's family, linking financial stewardship with the practice of faith and caring for those entrusted to our care.

Ecclesiastes 7:12 (NIV):

"Wisdom is a shelter as money is a shelter, but the advantage of knowledge is this: Wisdom preserves those who have it."

This verse from Ecclesiastes draws a parallel between the value of wisdom and the value of money as shelters. However, it ultimately highlights the enduring advantage of knowledge and wisdom, which can lead to preserving and enriching our lives in ways that material wealth alone cannot.

Once I understood what the problems were, I knew I needed to figure out the process of making a change for the better. There was always more month than money. I always seemed to lack. I began paying attention to those who were successful. I wanted to be like them. I knew I needed to see what they were doing that I had not yet mastered. It is never too late to change your path. It is never too late to change the trajectory of your life. If we change nothing, nothing will change. Making a decision and understanding that things were not working as is, was the best assessment and journey I could ever embark on. The decision wasn't easy, but it was necessary. I took a deep breath, faced the mirror, and made a commitment to myself. It was time to reassess, strategize, and take control of my financial destiny. Armed with determination, I started researching, cutting unnecessary expenses, and exploring new opportunities. It was a daunting journey, but the prospect of a more stable and fulfilling financial future fueled my resolve. Little did I know that this realization would be the catalyst for a transformative chapter in my life.

With each step towards financial introspection, I confronted the hard truths that had been lingering in the shadows for too long. I began to scrutinize my spending habits, distinguishing between necessities and indulgences. The process demanded a level of honesty that was uncomfortable, yet liberating. As I meticulously reviewed my budget, I discovered areas where I could trim excess and redirect funds towards meaningful goals. Sacrifices were inevitable, but they were investments in my future stability. The daunting task of creating a new financial plan forced me to set clear objectives, establish a realistic timeline, and cultivate a disciplined approach to money management.

The first few weeks were challenging, as breaking old habits and adjusting to a leaner lifestyle required resilience. I sought guidance from financial experts, devoured books on personal finance, and tapped into online communities that shared valuable insights. Embracing a proactive mindset, I explored additional income streams and side hustles. The initial discomfort of stepping out of my comfort zone soon transformed into a sense of empowerment.

The journey wasn't without setbacks, and there were moments when self-doubt crept in. However, the desire for change and the vision of a brighter financial future fueled my determination. As I navigated this uncharted territory, I discovered the strength within myself to adapt, learn, and grow. Life's financial challenges became a catalyst for personal growth, transforming what initially felt like a crisis into an opportunity for reinvention.

I found solace in the support of friends and family who understood the gravity of my situation. Opening up about my struggles was a vulnerable yet crucial step. Their encouragement and shared experiences reassured me that I wasn't alone in this journey. Together, we brainstormed ideas, exchanged advice, and celebrated small victories. It became a collective effort, reinforcing the idea that overcoming financial challenges wasn't solely an individual pursuit.

As the weeks turned into months, a palpable shift occurred. I witnessed the tangible results of my efforts. The overdue bills gradually transformed into paid statements, the budget began to balance, and the weight of financial uncertainty lifted. It wasn't a quick fix, but a slow and steady progression towards stability.

More than just a change in numbers on a spreadsheet, this process became a transformative chapter in my life. I not only learned the importance of fiscal responsibility but also discovered the resilience that resides within me. The journey taught me that life's challenges, when confronted head-on, can be stepping stones toward personal evolution. The decision to acknowledge the need for change was not just about my finances; it was a commitment to a more intentional and empowered way of living. As I embraced this newfound wisdom, I realized that the true essence of wealth lies not only in monetary abundance but in the lessons learned and the strength gained through facing life's adversities.

Moreover, this financial awakening rippled into other facets of my life. The discipline cultivated in budgeting spilled over into improved time management and a heightened awareness of my overall well-being. I started prioritizing self-care, recognizing that a healthy mind and body are invaluable assets. The change wasn't just about dollars and cents; it was about reclaiming control over my narrative.

The shift in mindset prompted me to set long-term goals and envision a future that extended beyond immediate financial concerns. I began investing in education and skill development, understanding that personal growth was a key component of sustained prosperity. The notion of financial freedom took on a broader meaning, encompassing not only economic stability but also the freedom to pursue passions and cultivate a fulfilling life.

In retrospect, the financial hardship that initially seemed like an insurmountable obstacle turned out to be a catalyst for a more profound transformation. It wasn't just about weathering the storm; it was about learning to dance in the rain. The resilience and resourcefulness I developed during this period became assets that extended far beyond the realm of finance. Each calculated step towards financial stability was, in essence, a stride towards a more purposeful and empowered existence.

The Warren Buffett Mindset

In the vast landscape of financial titans, there emerges a figure whose influence extends far beyond the realm of Wall Street, a man who I admire and whose wisdom and success have become the bedrock for aspiring investors and enthusiasts alike. This chapter embarks on a journey into the world of Warren Buffett, the Oracle of Omaha, exploring the reasons why he stands as an icon and a guiding light for countless individuals seeking financial acumen and success. Some may find it fascinating that I even know who he is. Not only do I know who he is, I know a great deal about his business model and financial sense.

The Humble Beginning

Warren Edward Buffett, born in 1930, began his journey in the humble city of Omaha, Nebraska. His early years were marked by an innate curiosity about the world of business, and it wasn't long before he began showcasing an uncanny ability to understand the complexities of financial markets. From delivering newspapers to making early investments in stocks, Buffett's journey was a testament to the power of determination and self-education.

The Principles of Value Investing

At the core of Warren Buffett's success lies the philosophy of value investing. Unlike many of his contemporaries who chased short-term gains, Buffett focused on identifying undervalued companies with strong fundamentals and a competitive edge. His adherence to timeless principles, such as investing in businesses he understood and holding stocks for the long term, sets him apart as a sage in the investment world.

The Wisdom of Patience

One of the most admirable traits of Warren Buffett is his unwavering patience. In an era dominated by the frenzy of quick gains and rapid trading, Buffett's ability to withstand market fluctuations and remain steadfast in his investment strategies is a beacon of inspiration. His famous quote, "The stock market is a device for transferring money from the impatient to the patient," encapsulates the essence of his approach.

A Lifetime of Learning

Warren Buffett's voracious appetite for knowledge is another facet that commands admiration. His commitment to continuous learning, from devouring financial reports to studying economic trends, underscores the importance of staying informed in the ever-evolving financial landscape. Buffett's annual letters to shareholders, filled with insights and reflections, serve as a masterclass for anyone aspiring to navigate the complexities of investments.

The Philanthropic Legacy

Beyond his financial prowess, Warren Buffett's commitment to philanthropy is a testament to his character. In tandem with Bill and Melinda Gates, he founded the Giving Pledge, a commitment by some of the world's wealthiest individuals to give away the majority of their wealth to address society's most pressing problems. Buffett's dedication to making a positive impact amplifies his influence far beyond the stock market.

The Personal Connection

As I delve into the life and principles of Warren Buffett, I find a personal connection that transcends the numbers on financial statements. His humility, wit, and genuine love for the craft of investing resonate with me on a profound level. Through the pages of his biographies, annual letters, and timeless quotes, I glean insights that extend beyond finance, offering valuable life lessons and perspectives.

My admiration for Warren Buffett goes beyond the numbers and charts. It's rooted in the principles of integrity, patience, and lifelong learning that have defined his remarkable journey. Through this exploration, I aim to distill the essence of his success into actionable insights, paving the way for my own financial journey guided by the wisdom of the Oracle of Omaha.

Embracing the Buffett Mindset

To fully embrace the Buffett mindset is to embrace a holistic approach to life and wealth. It's not merely about financial gain; it's about understanding the underlying principles that drive success and applying them in every facet of one's journey. As I absorb the wisdom imparted by Buffett, I am compelled to integrate these principles into my own life, creating a roadmap that extends beyond financial success.

The Long-Term Vision

Buffett's ability to look beyond the immediate fluctuations of the market and maintain a steadfast focus on the long term is a quality that resonates deeply with me. In a world dominated by instant gratification, adopting the long-term vision means cultivating the patience to weather storms and the discipline to adhere to a well-thought-out plan. It is a perspective that extends far beyond the stock market, influencing decisions in career, relationships, and personal development.

Risk, Reward, and Rationality

Buffett's approach to risk is not one of reckless abandon but of calculated analysis. He once remarked, "Risk comes from not knowing what you're doing," highlighting the importance of thorough research and understanding in mitigating risks. This rational approach to decision-making is a beacon in a world often swayed by emotions and speculative fervor. It encourages a methodical assessment of opportunities and a recognition of the relationship between risk and reward.

Building a Circle of Competence

A key tenet of Buffett's investment strategy is to stay within one's "circle of competence." This principle advises against venturing into unknown territories and instead encourages a deep understanding of the industries and businesses one invests in. Applying this concept to life, it becomes a guiding principle for making informed decisions, pursuing endeavors aligned with one's strengths, and continually expanding one's knowledge base.

Adapting to Change

While Buffett is renowned for his adherence to timeless principles, he is not resistant to change. His ability to adapt to new market dynamics and technologies showcases a flexibility that is crucial in any journey. It's a reminder that, even in the pursuit of long-term goals, the ability to evolve and embrace innovation is paramount.

Mentorship from Afar

Warren Buffett, through his writings, speeches, and interviews, becomes a virtual mentor, offering guidance to those willing to listen and learn. The invaluable lessons gleaned from his experiences become a source of inspiration, steering my financial decisions and life choices. It's a mentorship from afar, illustrating that wisdom transcends physical proximity and can be acquired through the thoughtful study of the experiences of those who came before.

In essence, my admiration for Warren Buffett extends beyond the financial realm. It's a recognition of a philosophy that encapsulates integrity, patience, and lifelong learning. As I embark on my own journey, I strive to embody these principles, weaving the wisdom of the Oracle of Omaha into the fabric of my aspirations and endeavors. Through this ongoing exploration, I aim not only to emulate financial success but to cultivate a mindset that enriches every facet of life.

Embracing Diversity in Wisdom

Warren Buffett's teachings resonate across boundaries, transcending differences in race, gender, and background. As a black female, I find a profound connection with the Oracle of Omaha, recognizing that wisdom knows no color or gender. Buffett's principles are not exclusive; they are universal truths that echo the values instilled in all of us as children of God.

Breaking Down Barriers

While Buffett may be a white male and I a black female, the fundamental principles of financial success and personal growth do not discriminate. Buffett's advice to avoid putting all your eggs in one basket is a universal truth that resonates with the essence of prudence. It became a catalyst for change in my life, prompting me to diversify my pursuits and not limit my potential based on preconceived notions or societal expectations.

A Shared Journey

In recognizing our shared humanity, I find inspiration in Buffett's journey—his struggles, triumphs, and the invaluable lessons learned along the way. As I navigate my own path, I draw strength from the notion that, irrespective of our backgrounds, we all face challenges and opportunities. Buffett's wisdom becomes a guiding light, offering insights that are applicable to anyone, regardless of race or gender.

Wisdom Beyond Stereotypes

Warren Buffett's success story challenges stereotypes and underscores the power of wisdom to dismantle barriers. His advice on investment strategies, risk management, and patience is not tailored to a specific demographic but is universally applicable. In learning from Buffett, I embrace the idea that wisdom is an equalizer, capable of inspiring positive change in the lives of individuals from all walks of life.

Beyond Surface Differences

As I absorb the teachings of Warren Buffett, I am reminded that our shared humanity unites us in a journey of growth and self-discovery. The superficial differences in race and gender fade away in the light of universal principles that guide financial success and personal development. Buffett's wisdom becomes a bridge, connecting diverse individuals in a shared pursuit of knowledge and prosperity.

The Light Bulb Moment

Buffett's timeless advice not to put all your eggs in one basket became a pivotal moment of realization for me. It sparked a change in my life, prompting a reassessment of my choices and a commitment to diversify my endeavors. This shift in perspective, inspired by the Oracle of Omaha, illustrates the transformative power of wisdom, irrespective of the background from which it emanates.

Now that I've explained why I admire Warren Buffett and his contributions to not only inspiring me personally, but also his contribution to the world. I will share what those contributions and his achievements look like.

Buffett's emphasis on diversification stems from the idea that spreading investments across different assets can help mitigate risks. By holding a variety of investments, the impact of a poor-performing asset on the overall portfolio is less severe. If one investment underperforms or faces challenges, the success of other investments can compensate for those losses.

Buffett's approach to investing is rooted in the principle of value investing, which involves carefully analyzing the fundamentals of a company before investing and holding onto investments for the long term. He is known for seeking companies with strong economic moats, sustainable competitive advantages, and competent management.

In terms of putting all your eggs in one basket, Buffett's warning is a caution against over-concentration in a single investment, industry, or asset class. The idea is to avoid excessive risk that could potentially wipe out a significant portion of your wealth if the chosen investment doesn't perform well.

It's important to note that while diversification is generally considered a prudent strategy, individual investment decisions should be based on one's financial goals, risk tolerance, and time horizon. The exact advice or statements from Warren Buffett may vary, so for the most accurate and up-to-date information, it's recommended to refer to his latest interviews, writings, or annual shareholder letters.

Buffett's strategy involves a focus on businesses with enduring competitive advantages, strong management teams, and a long-term perspective. He often highlights the importance of staying within one's circle of competence and not venturing into areas where one lacks expertise.

While diversification can be seen as a risk management strategy, Buffett's emphasis on knowing what you're doing suggests that blindly spreading investments across numerous assets without a solid understanding of each may not be the most effective approach.

Warren Buffett's financial portfolio, managed through his conglomerate Berkshire Hathaway, is a prime example of diversification and multiple sources of income.

Firstly, Berkshire Hathaway itself is a diversified holding company with investments in various sectors, including insurance, energy, utilities, consumer brands, and financial services. This diversification across industries helps buffer the company from the impact of economic downturns in any specific sector.

One significant component of Berkshire Hathaway's portfolio is its equity holdings in a range of publicly traded companies. Buffett and his team carefully select these investments based on the long-term potential of the businesses. These holdings cover diverse industries, including technology, finance, consumer goods, and healthcare. The idea is to have exposure to businesses with different economic sensitivities, reducing the overall risk associated with any single sector's performance.

Moreover, Berkshire Hathaway has a substantial presence in the insurance industry. Insurance operations, such as GEICO, provide a consistent stream of income through premiums collected. This aspect of the business operates as a stabilizing force, generating cash flows that can be reinvested or used for other strategic purposes.

In addition to equities and insurance, Berkshire Hathaway has invested in wholly-owned subsidiaries, which include companies engaged in manufacturing, energy, and retail. These subsidiaries contribute to the conglomerate's overall revenue and profitability, adding another layer of diversification.

Buffett's approach is not about frequent buying and selling but rather holding onto quality businesses for the long term. This patient and strategic investment philosophy has been a key factor in Berkshire Hathaway's success and its ability to generate income from various sources.

It's important to note that the specifics of Warren Buffett's portfolio can change, and for the latest information, one should refer to Berkshire Hathaway's annual shareholder letters, quarterly reports, and Buffett's interviews or statements. Always consider the most recent information when assessing an investor's portfolio strategy.

Furthermore, Warren Buffett's emphasis on investing in companies with strong economic moats contributes to the resilience and stability of his portfolio. Economic moats refer to a company's sustainable competitive advantages that protect it from competition and allow it to maintain high profitability over time. By focusing on businesses with wide economic moats, Buffett seeks to ensure that the companies in his portfolio have a durable competitive edge, which can weather market fluctuations and economic challenges.

The cash-generating capabilities of many of Berkshire Hathaway's investments also play a crucial role in sustaining the diversified income streams. The company often holds a significant amount of cash and cash equivalents, providing liquidity for potential investments, acquisitions, or weathering market downturns.

Buffett's approach to dividends is noteworthy as well. While many investors seek dividends for income, Berkshire Hathaway traditionally has not paid dividends. Instead, the company prefers to reinvest earnings into businesses that offer growth potential. This approach aligns with Buffett's long-term perspective, aiming for capital appreciation over time.

The multiple sources of income within Berkshire Hathaway's portfolio create a balanced and resilient financial structure. Whether through equity investments, insurance operations, or wholly-owned subsidiaries, the conglomerate benefits from a diversified revenue stream. This diversification not only helps mitigate risks associated with specific industries but also positions the portfolio to capitalize on opportunities across different sectors.

Warren Buffett, often referred to as the "Oracle of Omaha," is widely regarded as one of the most successful investors and business leaders in the world. While he has not been a traditional CEO or entrepreneur in the sense of building and running companies, his influence on America's business landscape is significant. Here are a few ways Warren Buffett's example and business standards have influenced America:

Long-Term Investing Philosophy:

> Warren Buffett is known for his long-term investment approach. He often emphasizes the importance of holding onto quality investments for extended periods. This philosophy has had an impact on the investment culture in America, encouraging

investors to focus on the long-term success and fundamentals of companies rather than short-term market fluctuations.

Value Investing Principles:

Buffett is a proponent of value investing, which involves identifying undervalued stocks and investing in them for the long term. This approach has influenced many investors and fund managers, contributing to the popularity of value investing strategies across the financial industry.

Emphasis on Business Fundamentals:

Buffett's success is often attributed to his deep understanding of business fundamentals. His emphasis on analyzing a company's financial health, competitive advantage, and management quality has encouraged a more rigorous and analytical approach to investing and business management.

Transparency and Communication:

Buffett is known for his straightforward communication style and emphasis on transparency. His annual letters to shareholders and public appearances have set an example for corporate leaders in terms of open communication with stakeholders. This has contributed to a broader trend of increased transparency and communication within the business world.

Corporate Governance:

Buffett has been vocal about the importance of strong corporate governance. His influence has, in part, contributed to increased awareness and efforts to improve corporate governance practices in America. Companies are now under greater scrutiny regarding issues such as executive compensation, board independence, and shareholder rights.

Philanthropy and Giving Pledge:

Warren Buffett, along with Bill and Melinda Gates, initiated the Giving Pledge, encouraging billionaires to commit the majority of their wealth to philanthropy. This initiative has influenced a number of wealthy individuals in America to publicly commit to giving away a significant portion of their wealth for charitable purposes.

Cultural Impact:

Buffett's folksy and down-to-earth demeanor, despite his immense wealth, has made him a unique and relatable figure. His lifestyle choices, such as living in the same house for many years and driving a modest car, have influenced perceptions of success and wealth in American culture.

While Buffett's impact on America's business standards is notable, it's essential to recognize that the business landscape is shaped by a multitude of factors and individuals. Buffett's principles, however, have certainly left an enduring mark on investment philosophy, corporate behavior, and philanthropy in the United States.

Buffett's leadership at Berkshire Hathaway has turned the conglomerate into a model for long-term success and value creation. The company's approach to acquiring and managing businesses, along with its decentralized structure, has been studied and emulated by other companies. Berkshire's annual shareholder meetings, known as the "Woodstock for Capitalists," have become a forum for sharing insights and learning from Buffett's experiences.

Warren Buffett's impact on America's business culture is multifaceted, encompassing investment strategies, corporate behavior, leadership principles, and societal responsibilities. His example continues to shape the mindset of investors, business leaders, and entrepreneurs, influencing decisions and strategies across various sectors.

I will always have great respect for Warren Buffett. He is getting older and I'm sure even wiser. The influence and contributions his genius left on America is invaluable.

Earvin Magic Johnson

Earvin "Magic" Johnson's impact on America as a businessman transcends his legendary basketball career and has left an indelible mark on the business world. Since retiring from professional basketball, Magic Johnson has emerged as a successful entrepreneur and influential figure in the business community. His charismatic personality and strategic acumen have allowed him to build an empire that spans various industries, including entertainment, real estate, and sports. Magic has been a trailblazer in promoting diversity and inclusion in business, particularly through his investments in urban communities and minority-owned enterprises. His Magic Johnson Enterprises has played a pivotal role in revitalizing underserved neighborhoods, creating job opportunities, and fostering economic development. Through partnerships with major corporations, Magic has demonstrated the power of collaboration in driving positive social and economic change. As a visionary businessman, philanthropist, and advocate for diversity, Magic Johnson continues to inspire future generations, proving that success in business can be a force for positive transformation in America.

Magic Johnson's influence extends beyond the boardroom, as he has become a sought-after motivational speaker and mentor. Leveraging his own experiences and challenges, he encourages aspiring entrepreneurs and young professionals to pursue their dreams with resilience and determination. Magic's commitment to education and empowerment is evident in initiatives like the Magic Johnson Foundation, which focuses on providing educational opportunities, scholarships, and resources to underserved communities. His philanthropic efforts underscore his dedication to creating lasting social change and addressing systemic inequalities. Magic Johnson's multifaceted impact on America as a businessman, mentor, and philanthropist showcases the transformative potential of combining business success with a commitment to social responsibility. In doing so, he has not only shaped the business landscape but also contributed significantly to building a more inclusive and equitable society.

Magic Johnson has been a catalyst for change in the sports ownership landscape. His ownership stake in the Los Angeles Lakers, one of the most iconic franchises in the NBA, marked a groundbreaking moment as he became one of the few African American majority owners in professional sports. Through this role, Magic has not only brought a winning mentality to the team but has also championed diversity within the upper echelons of sports management. His leadership has set a precedent for increased representation of minorities in ownership positions across major sports leagues, inspiring a new generation of leaders to break barriers in the sports industry.

In addition to his contributions to sports and business, Magic Johnson has also embraced technology and innovation. His investments in tech start-ups and ventures demonstrate a forward-thinking approach, showing that he is not only adept at navigating traditional industries but is also keen on staying at the forefront of emerging trends. By embracing the intersection of sports, entertainment, and technology, Magic Johnson continues to be a visionary force, shaping the landscape of American business in the 21st century.

In summary, Magic Johnson's influence on America as a businessman is multifaceted, encompassing not only his entrepreneurial success but also his commitment to social causes, his impact on sports ownership diversity, and his embrace of innovation. His legacy serves as an inspiration for individuals from all walks of life, showcasing the transformative power of business as a tool for positive change and inclusivity.

I am equally inspired by Magic Johnson and his example he has set financially and as a man of faith, a devoted husband and father. He is the epitome of financial success achieved with a diversified portfolio and not putting all of your eggs in one basket. Magic Johnson retired from the NBA in 1991 but has continued to make a significant impact in various industries.

Magic Johnson Enterprises (MJE): Magic Johnson formed Magic Johnson Enterprises, a company that serves as a conglomerate for his various business ventures. MJE has investments in a wide range of industries, including entertainment, real estate, food and beverage, and technology.

Real Estate: Magic Johnson has been involved in real estate development, particularly in urban areas. He has focused on revitalizing underserved communities by investing in commercial and residential developments.

Movie Theaters: One notable investment by Magic Johnson is in the movie theater business. He partnered with Sony Pictures to develop Magic Johnson Theatres, a chain of movie theaters designed to provide entertainment options in urban neighborhoods.

Franchising: Magic Johnson has been involved in franchising businesses, including Starbucks and 24 Hour Fitness. His investment in these franchises has contributed to their growth and success.

Sports Ownership: Magic Johnson has owned stakes in professional sports teams. He was a part-owner of the Los Angeles Lakers, and his involvement was instrumental in the team's success. He also had ownership stakes in Major League Baseball's Los Angeles Dodgers.

Health and Fitness: Magic Johnson has invested in health and fitness ventures, including partnerships with companies like 24 Hour Fitness. His focus on promoting a healthy lifestyle aligns with the growing awareness of fitness and wellness.

Technology Investments: Magic Johnson has explored investments in the technology sector. His diverse portfolio includes ventures in the tech industry, showcasing his adaptability to changing business landscapes.

Community Development: Magic Johnson has been actively involved in community development projects. His real estate investments often include projects aimed at revitalizing urban areas and providing economic opportunities for local residents.

Partnerships and Collaborations: Johnson has been known for forming strategic partnerships and collaborations with other successful entrepreneurs and companies. These partnerships have not only strengthened his ventures but also contributed to the overall success of the businesses involved.

Philanthropy: Magic Johnson has been engaged in philanthropic activities, supporting various charitable causes. His commitment to giving back to the community aligns with his focus on making a positive impact beyond the business realm.

Media and Entertainment: In addition to his involvement in movie theaters, Magic Johnson has explored ventures in the media and entertainment industry. This includes investments in television and radio stations, as well as content production.

Personal Branding: Magic Johnson's personal brand has played a crucial role in his business success. His reputation as a legendary basketball player and a successful entrepreneur has helped him attract opportunities and build trust with both consumers and business partners.

Advisory Roles: Magic Johnson has served in advisory roles and on boards for various companies. His insights and business acumen have been valued by organizations seeking strategic guidance.

Magic Johnson's philosophy on business is characterized by several key principles that have contributed to his success as an entrepreneur

Diversification: Magic Johnson emphasizes the importance of diversifying investments across various industries. By having a diverse portfolio, he reduces risk and taps into multiple revenue streams. This philosophy reflects his belief in the need for adaptability in the ever-changing business landscape.

Community Empowerment: Johnson is committed to making a positive impact on the communities he invests in. His business ventures often include projects aimed at community development, job creation, and economic revitalization. This reflects a philosophy of using business as a tool for social change and empowerment.

Identifying Underserved Markets: Magic Johnson has a keen eye for identifying and capitalizing on opportunities in underserved markets. Whether it's investing in urban real estate or bringing entertainment options to neglected neighborhoods, his philosophy involves recognizing potential where others may not.

Strategic Partnerships: Johnson believes in the power of collaboration and strategic partnerships. Throughout his business career, he has formed alliances with other successful entrepreneurs and companies to strengthen his ventures. Building strong partnerships has been a cornerstone of his business strategy.

Customer-Centric Approach: Magic Johnson places a strong emphasis on understanding and catering to the needs of his target audience. Whether in the fitness industry, entertainment, or real estate, he prioritizes creating businesses that resonate with and benefit the communities they serve.

Long-Term Vision: Johnson's business philosophy extends beyond short-term gains. He is known for taking a long-term view in his investments and projects. This approach involves patience, persistence, and a commitment to sustained success over time.

Adaptability: In the dynamic world of business, Magic Johnson advocates for adaptability. He has shown the ability to evolve with changing trends, technologies, and market demands. This flexibility is crucial for staying relevant and successful in the long run.

Personal Branding and Integrity: Magic Johnson understands the value of personal branding and integrity in business. His reputation as a basketball legend and a trustworthy entrepreneur has played a significant role in attracting opportunities and building lasting relationships.

Magic continues to make power moves and leave an incredible legacy.

Mary Kay Ash

When I think about a powerhouse, the late Mary Kay Ash comes to mind. She has undeniably changed the scope of direct marketing and business for so many successful women. I absolutely love the Mary Kay products and have always been inspired by her business philosophy. She never put all of her eggs into one basket.

Mary Kay Ash (1918–2001) was an American businesswoman and the founder of Mary Kay Cosmetics, a multi-level marketing company that specializes in cosmetics and skincare products. She started the company in 1963 with the goal of providing women with an opportunity to achieve financial success while balancing family life. Mary Kay Ash was a trailblazer in the male-dominated business world, and her company became one of the largest and most successful direct-selling beauty businesses in the world.

One of the key aspects of Mary Kay Ash's business model was diversification, which she achieved by implementing a multi-level marketing (MLM) strategy. In a traditional business model, a company sells products through retailers or distributors. In contrast, Mary Kay's MLM model involved direct selling, where independent beauty consultants sold products directly to consumers and also recruited others to become consultants. Consultants earned commissions not only from their own sales but also from the sales of those they recruited.

This multi-level structure allowed Mary Kay Cosmetics to diversify its sales channels and revenue streams. Instead of relying solely on traditional retail outlets, the company created a vast network of independent consultants who operated on a commission-based system. This approach had several benefits:

> Wider Market Reach: The MLM model allowed Mary Kay to reach a broader customer base through a decentralized network of consultants who could sell products directly to consumers in their local communities.
> Entrepreneurial Opportunity: By offering individuals the opportunity to become independent beauty consultants, Mary Kay created a flexible business model that empowered

women to start their own businesses without the need for significant upfront investment.

Resilience to Economic Changes: The diversification of sales channels made Mary Kay Cosmetics more resilient to economic fluctuations. While traditional retail businesses might be heavily affected by economic downturns, the direct selling model could adapt to changing market conditions.

Motivational Incentives: The MLM structure provided consultants with the opportunity to earn not only from their personal sales but also from the sales of their recruits. This created a motivational incentive for consultants to build and support their teams, fostering a sense of community and collaboration.

Mary Kay Ash's innovative business model and emphasis on empowering women in the business world have left a lasting legacy. While MLM models have faced criticism for certain practices, the success of Mary Kay Cosmetics and its impact on the cosmetics industry cannot be denied.

Mary Kay Ash's emphasis on empowering women and her commitment to creating a positive and supportive business environment were also key factors in the success of her business model. She believed in recognizing and rewarding the achievements of her consultants and implemented various motivational incentives within the company.

Some notable aspects of Mary Kay Cosmetics' business model and practices include:

Recognition and Rewards: Mary Kay implemented a system of recognition and rewards to motivate and celebrate the achievements of her consultants. The company introduced various awards, including the famous pink Cadillac, which became a symbol of success for top-performing consultants.

Training and Support: Mary Kay recognized the importance of training and supporting her consultants. The company provided extensive training programs, workshops, and educational materials to help consultants develop their business skills, product knowledge, and sales techniques.

Product Innovation: Mary Kay Cosmetics focused on continually innovating and expanding its product line to meet the evolving needs and preferences of its customers. This commitment to product quality and variety helped sustain the interest of both consultants and consumers.

Commitment to Ethics: Mary Kay emphasized ethical business practices and a commitment to integrity. This commitment helped build trust among consultants and customers, contributing to the long-term success and positive reputation of the company.

Community and Sisterhood: Mary Kay fostered a sense of community and sisterhood among the consultants. Regular events, meetings, and conferences provided opportunities for consultants to connect, share experiences, and support each other. This sense of community was a powerful motivator for consultants to stay engaged with the business.

While Mary Kay Ash's business model and strategies were successful, it's important to note that the MLM industry has faced scrutiny and controversy over the years. Critics have raised concerns about the sustainability of MLM structures, potential exploitation, and issues related to recruitment practices. As with any business model, there are both positive aspects and challenges associated with MLM, and perspectives on its effectiveness may vary.

Mary Kay Ash's legacy extends beyond her business success; she also became known for her philanthropy and efforts to empower women. The company continues to operate based on the principles she established, evolving with the times while maintaining its focus on empowering individuals, particularly women, through entrepreneurial opportunities in the beauty industry.

Mary Kay Ash's business philosophy, often encapsulated in her famous quote "God first, family second, career third," reflected her values and priorities. She believed in creating a business environment that emphasized not only financial success but also personal fulfillment and balance in life. Here are key elements of Mary Kay Ash's business philosophy:

> Prioritizing Values: Mary Kay believed in placing faith, family, and personal values at the forefront. By encouraging her consultants to prioritize their spiritual and family lives, she aimed to create a business model that supported a well-rounded and fulfilling lifestyle.
>
> Empowering Others: Central to Mary Kay's philosophy was the idea of empowering individuals, especially women, to

achieve their full potential. She wanted to provide opportunities for women to build successful businesses while maintaining control over their schedules and family lives.

Positive Reinforcement: Mary Kay was a proponent of positive reinforcement and recognition. She understood the importance of acknowledging and celebrating the achievements of her consultants, fostering a positive and uplifting atmosphere within the company.

Equality and Inclusivity: Mary Kay Ash was a pioneer in promoting equality and inclusivity. She built a company where women could succeed based on their abilities, regardless of traditional gender norms prevalent in the business world at the time.

Golden Rule Philosophy: Mary Kay often spoke about the "Golden Rule" philosophy, encouraging consultants to treat others as they would like to be treated. This principle underscored the importance of fairness, integrity, and ethical conduct in business relationships.

Balancing Professional and Personal Lives: Mary Kay's philosophy emphasized the importance of finding a balance between professional and personal aspects of life. This resonated with many individuals who sought not only financial success but also a sense of purpose and fulfillment beyond their careers.

Continuous Improvement: Mary Kay believed in continuous improvement and personal development. Her company provided extensive training and educational resources to help consultants enhance their skills and knowledge, contributing to their growth both personally and professionally.

Mary Kay Ash's unique blend of business acumen and a values-driven approach set her apart as a leader in the cosmetics industry. Her philosophy not only shaped the culture of Mary Kay Cosmetics but also influenced the broader conversation about women in business and the potential for entrepreneurship to empower individuals in all aspects of their lives.

Cathy Hughes

When I think of the definition of a shero, Cafhy Hughes comes to mind. I am highly familiar with Television production and the intricate details of radio because of my music. I am so proud of her longevity and her business genius. I first learned of Cathy when I was selected to be a cast member of a faith based Reality show with other famous and notable women of faith. According to our executive producer, our show made it all the way to the TV One executives, but did not make the final cut. However, my awareness of who the owner of this amazing company was influenced my life greatly.

TV One is a television network in the United States that primarily targets African American and African audiences. It was launched in January 2004. TV One was founded by Cathy Hughes, an entrepreneur and media personality. Cathy Hughes is also the founder and chairperson of Urban One, Inc., the parent company of TV One.

Cathy Hughes is a prominent figure in the media industry, and her business philosophy involves creating content that caters to diverse audiences, particularly those underserved by mainstream media. Urban One, Inc. has a diversified portfolio that includes radio, digital media, and television properties, with a focus on providing a platform for African American and urban communities. The company aims to address the unique interests and perspectives of its target audience through its various media outlets.

Cathy Hughes has been a trailblazer in the media industry, particularly in promoting diversity and inclusion. Through Urban One, Inc., she has built a media empire that reaches millions of people across different platforms.

The business model of TV One involves creating and broadcasting a range of content, including original programming, movies, news, and lifestyle shows, that reflects the interests and experiences of its target audience. The network strives to provide a platform for underrepresented voices and stories, contributing to a more inclusive media landscape.

Urban One, Inc.'s diversified portfolio extends beyond TV One and includes a network of radio stations, digital media properties, and other ventures. This diversification allows the company to reach audiences through multiple channels and adapt to the evolving media landscape.

Cathy Hughes has been recognized for her contributions to the media industry and her commitment to promoting diversity. Her business philosophy emphasizes the importance of empowering and amplifying the voices of African Americans and other marginalized communities.

Cathy Hughes's contributions extend beyond TV One, and she is notably associated with Radio One, now known as Urban One, Inc., which she founded with her son, Alfred Liggins III. Radio One is a media company that focuses on radio broadcasting, targeting primarily African American and urban audiences.

Radio One, under Cathy Hughes's leadership, became the largest African American-owned and operated broadcast company in the United States. The company owns and operates a network of radio stations across the country, providing a platform for diverse voices and serving communities that may be underserved by mainstream media.

Cathy Hughes's innovative approach in the radio industry included acquiring underperforming radio stations and transforming them into profitable ventures by tailoring the content to the local communities. This strategy not only contributed to the success of Radio One but also helped amplify the voices of minority communities.

Furthermore, Urban One, Inc. expanded its presence into digital media, reaching audiences through online platforms and contributing to the company's overall diversified portfolio. Cathy Hughes's business contributions, both in radio and television, have played a significant role in shaping the landscape of African American-focused media in the United States. Her dedication to providing a platform for underrepresented communities has left a lasting impact on the media industry.

Cathy Hughes's business strategy demonstrates a clear commitment to not putting all her eggs in one basket. Instead of focusing solely on one aspect of the media industry, she has diversified her business portfolio across various platforms, showcasing her foresight and adaptability in the ever-evolving media landscape.

> Radio Broadcasting: Cathy Hughes started with a strong foothold in radio through the founding of Radio One (now Urban One, Inc.). This move allowed her to tap into the unique and intimate connection that radio has with local communities, particularly those that were often underserved by mainstream media.
>
> Television Broadcasting: Recognizing the potential to reach a broader audience and provide more diverse content,

Hughes expanded into television with the creation of TV One. This move allowed her to leverage the visual medium to tell stories, showcase diverse perspectives, and connect with a broader viewer base.

Digital Media: Understanding the shift in consumer behavior towards digital platforms, Urban One, Inc. expanded into digital media, reaching audiences through online platforms. This move not only aligned with changing media consumption habits but also positioned the company to engage with younger, tech-savvy demographics.

By diversifying her business across radio, television, and digital media, Cathy Hughes has created a robust and adaptable media empire. This strategy not only mitigates risks associated with changes in consumer preferences but also ensures that Urban One, Inc. has a presence across various channels, reaching a wide spectrum of audiences. It reflects a business philosophy that embraces diversity not only in content but also in the means of delivering that content to the audience.

Sheila Johnson

When I think of excellence and grace, this regal lady comes to mind. Sheila Johnson also exudes confidence and sound business sense.

Sheila Johnson is a successful businesswoman known for co-founding BET (Black Entertainment Television) and for her contributions to the hospitality and sports industries.

Here's a brief overview of Sheila Johnson's background:

Co-founder of BET: Sheila Johnson, along with her former husband Robert L. Johnson and others, co-founded BET in 1980. BET grew to become the first black-controlled company listed on the New York Stock Exchange.

Sports Ventures: In addition to her involvement in media, Sheila Johnson is known for her contributions to the sports industry. She is the only African-American woman to have ownership in three professional sports teams: the Washington Wizards (NBA), the Washington Capitals (NHL), and the Washington Mystics (WNBA).

Hospitality: Sheila Johnson is also a successful entrepreneur in the hospitality sector. She is the founder and CEO of Salamander Hotels & Resorts, a luxury hotel company. The company owns and operates several upscale properties, including the Salamander Resort & Spa in Virginia.

In terms of business philosophy, Sheila Johnson has emphasized the importance of diversity and inclusion. She has been an advocate for women's rights and has actively participated in various philanthropic efforts.

Salamander Resort & Spa, Virginia:
- Located in Middleburg, Virginia, the Salamander Resort & Spa is a luxury property known for its upscale amenities and picturesque surroundings.

- The resort offers a range of recreational activities, including a spa, equestrian facilities, fine dining, and more.
- It has been recognized for its commitment to providing a high-end and immersive experience for guests.

Other Potential Locations:
- Salamander Hotels & Resorts has expanded its portfolio beyond the Salamander Resort & Spa in Virginia. Additional properties may include resorts and hotels in various locations, offering unique experiences and services.

Sheila Johnson's business philosophy is characterized by several key principles, including diversity, resilience, and a strategic approach to investments. One aspect of her philosophy is the belief in not putting all of her eggs in one basket, which aligns with the idea of diversification. Here are some points that reflect Sheila Johnson's business philosophy:

Diversity and Inclusion:
- Sheila Johnson has been a strong advocate for diversity and inclusion, both in the workplace and in the media industry. She believes in creating opportunities for individuals from different backgrounds and promoting equality.

Resilience and Overcoming Challenges:
- Throughout her career, Sheila Johnson has faced challenges and setbacks, but she has demonstrated resilience in overcoming them. She believes in learning from failures and using them as stepping stones to future success.

Strategic Investments:
- The notion of not putting all of her eggs in one basket reflects a strategy of diversification. Sheila Johnson has applied this principle to her business ventures, with involvement in various industries such as media, sports, and hospitality.

Entrepreneurial Spirit:
- Sheila Johnson is known for her entrepreneurial spirit, having co-founded BET and later establishing herself in the hospitality industry with Salamander Hotels & Resorts. Her willingness to explore different sectors showcases an openness to new opportunities and challenges.

Philanthropy:
- Johnson has also been actively involved in philanthropy, supporting causes related to education, health, and the arts. Her commitment to making a positive impact extends beyond business ventures.

Leadership and Mentorship:

- As a successful businesswoman, Sheila Johnson emphasizes the importance of leadership and mentorship. She has been a role model for aspiring entrepreneurs and has contributed to fostering talent in various fields.

Overall, Sheila Johnson's business philosophy is grounded in a combination of strategic decision-making, resilience, and a commitment to making a positive impact on both the business world and society at large.

Celebrities Who Get It

Many celebrities diversify their financial portfolios and invest in various ventures beyond their primary entertainment careers.

While specific information about celebrities' financial portfolios is often private, here are some examples of celebrities known for their successful investments and diverse business interests:

Ashton Kutcher: Kutcher is a well-known tech investor who has invested in companies like Airbnb, Uber, and Spotify through his venture capital firm, A-Grade Investments.

Jessica Alba: The actress co-founded The Honest Company, a consumer goods company focused on non-toxic household products. The company has been successful and went public in 2021.

George Clooney: Clooney and his business partners sold their tequila company, Casamigos, to Diageo for $1 billion in 2017. The actor has also been involved in various real estate investments.

Oprah Winfrey: Beyond her successful media career, Oprah has invested in Weight Watchers and has a significant stake in the OWN network. She's known for her diverse business ventures and investments.

Mark Wahlberg: The actor and producer has expanded into various business ventures, including a successful career as a film and television producer, co-ownership of the Wahlburgers restaurant chain, and investments in fitness and nutritional products.

Ellen DeGeneres: Comedian and talk show host Ellen DeGeneres has a production company and has invested in real estate. She also has interests in lifestyle brands and products.

LeBron James: The NBA superstar has invested in various businesses, including Blaze Pizza, SpringHill Entertainment, and a stake in Liverpool FC. LeBron is known for his strategic investments and business acumen.

Serena Williams: Tennis champion Serena Williams has ventured into business with investments in fashion and tech startups. She is also the founder of Serena Ventures, which focuses on early-stage investments in diverse industries.

Ryan Reynolds: The actor and entrepreneur Ryan Reynolds has made strategic investments outside of his acting career. He is a co-owner of Aviation American Gin, which was acquired by Diageo in 2020, and has been involved in other business ventures.

Nas: The rapper Nas is known for his investment in tech startups. He was an early investor in companies like Ring, Lyft, and Dropbox, showcasing his interest in the technology sector.

Gwyneth Paltrow: Actress Gwyneth Paltrow is not only known for her work in Hollywood but also as the founder of the lifestyle and wellness brand Goop. The brand has expanded into various product categories and has become a significant part of Paltrow's entrepreneurial endeavors.

Robert Downey Jr.: Known for his role as Iron Man in the Marvel Cinematic Universe, Robert Downey Jr. has expanded his interests beyond acting. He has invested in tech startups and has been involved in the development of innovative technologies.

Tyra Banks: In addition to her successful modeling and television career, Tyra Banks has ventured into entrepreneurship. She founded TYRA Beauty, a cosmetics line, and has invested in various business ventures.

Dr. Dre: The legendary hip-hop producer and rapper, Dr. Dre, achieved notable success not only in music but also in business. He co-founded Beats by Dre, a high-end audio products company, which was later acquired by Apple Inc. for a significant sum.

Robert De Niro: The acclaimed actor Robert De Niro has not only excelled in the film industry but has also invested in the hospitality sector. He co-owns the Nobu restaurant chain and the Greenwich Hotel in New York.

Ellen Pompeo: Best known for her role in the long-running TV series "Grey's Anatomy," Ellen Pompeo has diversified her career by not only acting but also by producing and directing. She has been involved in various projects and has a production company, Calamity Jane.

Jessica Biel: Actress Jessica Biel has ventured into the wellness industry. She co-founded the wellness brand Au Fudge and is involved in advocating for health and environmental causes.

Dwayne "The Rock" Johnson: Beyond his successful wrestling and acting career, Dwayne Johnson has diversified his ventures. He has his own production company, Seven Bucks Productions, and is involved in business ventures ranging from fitness products to tequila.

Natalie Portman: Academy Award-winning actress Natalie Portman has not only pursued a successful acting career but has also ventured into entrepreneurship. She co-founded a venture capital firm, investing in startups that focus on social impact and innovation.

Leonardo DiCaprio: Known for his environmental activism, Leonardo DiCaprio has invested in environmentally friendly businesses and startups. He is also a co-founder of the environmental foundation, Earth Alliance.

These examples highlight how various celebrities have leveraged their success and fame to diversify their financial portfolios. Their investments span different industries, including technology, hospitality, beauty, and wellness, showcasing a strategic approach to financial planning beyond their primary careers in the entertainment industry.

Spread Your Eggs

The concept of not putting all your eggs in one basket is a metaphorical expression that underscores the importance of diversification and risk management. Just as placing all your eggs in a single basket makes them vulnerable to breaking if that basket falls, relying solely on one source of income or investment exposes you to a higher level of risk. The essence of this saying lies in spreading your assets, investments, and income streams across various avenues to minimize the impact of potential losses and enhance overall financial resilience.

In practical terms, it encourages individuals to explore different financial opportunities, such as investing in various assets, starting a side business, or pursuing multiple career paths. By doing so, one can better navigate economic uncertainties, industry fluctuations, and unexpected life events.

The principle of not putting all your eggs in one basket aligns with the philosophy of diversification, promoting a more robust and adaptive approach to managing personal finances and building wealth over time.

This principle is particularly relevant in a dynamic and ever-changing economic landscape. Markets fluctuate, industries evolve, and unforeseen challenges can arise. By diversifying one's financial portfolio and income streams, individuals can create a more resilient foundation. This approach not only safeguards against the potential impact of a downturn in a specific sector but also positions individuals to capitalize on emerging opportunities.

The philosophy of not putting all your eggs in one basket extends beyond financial considerations. It encourages a mindset of adaptability and foresight, emphasizing the importance of being proactive in managing one's resources. This mindset is applicable not only to investments but also to career choices, personal development, and lifestyle decisions.

For example, someone with diverse skills and experiences is better equipped to navigate changes in the job market or industry trends. Similarly, a person who explores various interests and hobbies is likely to find more fulfillment and balance in life. The overarching idea is to avoid over-reliance on a single strategy or avenue, recognizing that diversity can be a source of strength and resilience.

Not putting all your eggs in one basket is a guiding principle that advocates for a well-rounded and adaptable approach to life and finances. It promotes the idea that a diversified and balanced portfolio, whether in investments, career paths, or personal pursuits, can lead to greater stability, increased opportunities, and a more fulfilling life journey. By embracing this principle, individuals can position themselves to thrive in the face of uncertainty and actively shape their paths towards long-term success and well-being.

Furthermore, the principle of not putting all your eggs in one basket encourages a holistic view of risk and reward. It recognizes that different opportunities come with varying levels of uncertainty and potential return. By diversifying, individuals can optimize their risk-reward profile, balancing the stability of certain income sources with the growth potential of others.

This approach aligns with the broader concept of portfolio management, a strategy commonly employed in financial markets. Just as a well-diversified investment portfolio can better weather market volatility, a diversified set of income streams can provide stability during economic fluctuations and unexpected life events.

In the pursuit of financial success, it's essential to acknowledge that no single strategy or income source is foolproof. By diversifying, individuals not only spread risk but also position themselves to benefit from the strengths of different assets or ventures. For instance, while a stable job provides a consistent income, investments may offer opportunities for wealth accumulation and growth over time.

The principle emphasizes adaptability in the face of changing circumstances. As life unfolds, priorities shift, and new opportunities arise. Diversification allows individuals to pivot, take on new challenges, and explore avenues that align with their evolving goals and aspirations.

So, not putting all your eggs in one basket is a dynamic and forward-thinking approach to financial and life management. It reflects a recognition that diversity, both in income streams and life experiences, not only mitigates risks but also enhances the potential for sustained success and fulfillment. By embracing this principle, individuals can navigate the complexities of an ever-changing world with resilience, agility, and a greater capacity to seize opportunities as they arise.

Diversifying income sources provides individuals with a myriad of options and opportunities, fostering financial resilience and the potential for wealth creation. Relying on a single job or income stream places one at the mercy of economic uncertainties and industry fluctuations. By strategically spreading investments, engaging in side businesses, or exploring various passive income avenues, individuals can navigate challenges more effectively. This multifaceted approach not only mitigates risks but also opens doors to new possibilities. It allows for the pursuit of passions, the exploration of diverse interests, and the flexibility to adapt to changing circumstances. Creating wealth becomes a tangible prospect as the combined strength of multiple income streams contributes to a more stable and prosperous financial future. In essence, avoiding the "all eggs in one basket" scenario empowers individuals to seize opportunities, weather economic storms, and build a foundation for long-term financial success.

Here are some key benefits of not relying solely on one job and diversifying your sources of income:

> **Risk Mitigation:** Relying on a single source of income, such as a job, exposes you to a higher level of risk. If you were to lose that job or face economic challenges in that specific industry, your entire financial stability could be at risk. Diversifying your income streams helps mitigate this risk.
> **Financial Stability:** Multiple streams of income contribute to financial stability. If one source experiences a downturn,

others may compensate for the loss, helping you maintain a steady overall income.

Adaptability: Economic landscapes are dynamic, and industries can change rapidly. Diversifying your income allows you to adapt to changing circumstances. If one industry faces a decline, your other sources of income may be unaffected or less impacted.

Opportunity for Growth: Different income streams may offer varied opportunities for growth. While a job provides a fixed salary, other ventures such as investments, freelancing, or a side business can potentially yield higher returns and contribute to overall wealth accumulation.

Increased Financial Freedom: Having multiple streams of income can provide a greater sense of financial freedom. It may allow you to have more control over your time, pursue passion projects, or take risks that you might not be able to afford if you were solely dependent on one income source.

Skill Development: Diversifying income often involves acquiring new skills and knowledge. Whether it's investing, freelancing, or entrepreneurship, you may develop a broader skill set that enhances your overall employability and adaptability.

Retirement Planning: Diversification is crucial for long-term financial planning, especially in terms of retirement. Relying solely on a traditional job may not provide sufficient funds for a comfortable retirement. Diverse income streams can contribute to a more robust retirement savings portfolio.

It's important to note that diversification should be done strategically, taking into account your skills, interests, and risk tolerance. While having multiple income streams can offer numerous benefits, it also requires careful planning and management to ensure success

Here are some examples of how you might diversify your sources of income:

Primary Job or Career:
- Example: Working a full-time job in a corporate office, government agency, or any other industry.

Side Business:
- Example: Starting a small business on the side, such as a consulting service, online store, or freelance work in areas like graphic design, writing, or programming.

Investments:
- Example: Investing in stocks, bonds, mutual funds, real estate, or other financial instruments to generate passive income through dividends, interest, or capital gains.

Rental Income:
- Example: Owning property and renting it out for residential or commercial purposes.

Dividend Income:
- Example: Investing in dividend-paying stocks, where you receive a portion of the company's profits in the form of dividends.

Royalties:

- Example: Creating and monetizing intellectual property, such as writing books, composing music, or designing software, and earning royalties from the use of that property.

Online Ventures:
- Example: Generating income through online activities, such as affiliate marketing, sponsored content creation, or running a successful YouTube channel or blog.

Consulting or Coaching Services:
- Example: Offering your expertise as a consultant or coach on a part-time basis in areas such as business, career development, or personal finance.

Multiple Jobs or Freelancing:
- Example: Working part-time in addition to your full-time job or taking on freelance gigs in your spare time.

Real Estate Crowdfunding:
- Example: Investing in real estate through crowdfunding platforms, where you contribute funds alongside other investors for property development or rental projects.

Passive Income Streams:
- Example: Creating sources of passive income, such as automated online businesses, where you earn money without actively working on them once they're set up.

Educational Products:
- Example: Developing and selling educational products, such as online courses, ebooks, or tutorials, leveraging your expertise in a particular subject.

Remember, the key is to tailor your income diversification strategy to your skills, interests, and risk tolerance. A well-thought-out and diversified approach can provide greater financial security and flexibility over time.

Five Americans Who Got It

Amy's Story

Once upon a time in the small town of Willowville, there lived a determined and resilient woman named Amy. She was a single mother, raising her two children, Emily and Jake, with unwavering love and devotion. However, financial struggles had become a constant companion, and Amy found herself struggling to make ends meet.

Determined to provide a better life for her family, Amy decided to take matters into her own hands and explore various avenues to create additional streams of income.

First, she tapped into her passion for baking. Amy had always been known for her delicious homemade cookies and cakes. Recognizing the demand for homemade treats in her community, she began baking in larger quantities and offered her goods for sale at local events and farmers' markets. The delectable aroma of her baked goods quickly gained popularity, and soon, she had a steady stream of customers.

In addition to her baking venture, Amy discovered her talent for writing. She decided to start a blog, sharing her experiences as a single mother, offering parenting tips, and documenting her journey towards financial stability. As her blog gained traction, Amy monetized it through sponsored content and affiliate marketing, providing a consistent source of passive income.

To further diversify her income streams, Amy explored her artistic side. She had always enjoyed crafting, and she began creating handmade jewelry and accessories. Amy opened an online store to showcase her creations, reaching a wider audience beyond Willowville. The uniqueness of her designs attracted customers from different parts of the country, bringing in additional income.

Despite her busy schedule, Amy continued to seek opportunities for growth. She enrolled in online courses to enhance her skills in digital marketing and social media management. Armed with new knowledge, she offered consulting services to local businesses looking to establish a stronger online presence, further expanding her income streams.

As time passed, Amy's determination and hard work began to pay off. The combination of her baking business, successful blog, handmade jewelry store, and consulting services transformed her financial situation. She was able to provide a more comfortable life for Emily and Jake, ensuring they had access to educational opportunities and extracurricular activities.

Amy's story became an inspiration in Willowville, proving that with perseverance and creativity, one could overcome financial challenges. Her journey taught the community the importance of resilience and resourcefulness, inspiring others to explore their passions and talents to improve their own lives. In the end, Amy's unwavering spirit not only transformed her family's future but also became a beacon of hope for those facing similar struggles in Willowville.

Mark's Story

In the bustling city of Metroburg, there lived a determined and resourceful man named Mark. Despite his hard work, Mark found himself struggling to make ends meet in the expensive urban environment. Unfazed by the challenges, he decided to take control of his financial destiny and explore multiple streams of income.

Mark's first venture stemmed from his passion for fitness. Realizing the increasing demand for personalized training, he became a certified fitness instructor and started offering personal training sessions in local parks. His clients appreciated his dedication and motivational approach, and soon, Mark had a growing list of regulars.

In addition to his fitness business, Mark identified an opportunity in the gig economy. He signed up for various freelance platforms and began offering his skills in graphic design. With a natural talent for visual arts, Mark quickly gained a reputation for delivering high-quality designs, securing consistent freelance projects that added a substantial boost to his income.

As he navigated the world of freelancing, Mark discovered the potential of investing. Despite having limited funds, he educated himself on the basics of stock market investing and began putting aside a portion of his income to invest wisely. Over time, Mark's investment portfolio started to grow, providing him with a source of passive income that would prove valuable in the long run.

Realizing the power of the online world, Mark decided to share his journey and insights. He started a YouTube channel where he documented his experiences in fitness, freelancing, and investing. The channel gained a following as people resonated with his authenticity and practical advice. Mark monetized his channel through ads and sponsorships, creating another income stream.

To diversify further, Mark explored the booming world of e-commerce. He researched trending products and started an online store selling fitness-related merchandise. Leveraging his graphic design skills, he created unique and eye-catching designs that resonated with his audience. The online store became a success, contributing to Mark's growing financial stability.

Mark's determination and willingness to adapt continued to pay off. The combination of his fitness training, freelance graphic design, stock market investments, YouTube channel, and e-commerce store transformed his financial situation. He moved from living paycheck to paycheck to having a more secure and comfortable life in Metroburg.

Mark's story became an inspiration for others in the city, showcasing the possibilities that arise when one is open to exploring diverse income streams. His journey emphasized the importance of resilience, continuous learning, and leveraging one's skills to create financial stability. As Mark thrived in his newfound success, he became a living testament to the transformative power of determination and resourcefulness in the face of financial challenges.

The Johnson's Story

In the heart of New York City, where dreams and challenges collide, lived the Johnsons—a resilient couple determined to overcome the setbacks that led them to bankruptcy. Mark and Lisa Johnson, parents to three children, found themselves facing financial turmoil but were not willing to succumb to defeat.

After the bankruptcy filing, the couple sat down to assess their skills and passions. Mark had a background in IT, and Lisa was a talented artist. They decided to combine their strengths to create multiple streams of income.

Mark started by offering freelance IT consulting services. He reached out to local businesses and entrepreneurs in need of tech support and assistance with their systems. Through networking events and online platforms, he quickly gained clients, and his IT consulting business began to thrive.

Simultaneously, Lisa tapped into her artistic abilities. She set up an online store to sell her paintings and prints, showcasing her unique style inspired by the vibrant energy of New York City. Lisa also started offering art classes to children and adults, leveraging her skills to teach others while generating additional income.

Understanding the potential of the gig economy, Mark and Lisa explored platforms for short-term projects. Mark took on side gigs in website development, while Lisa accepted freelance graphic design projects. These endeavors not only brought in extra income but also expanded their professional networks.

The Johnsons were aware of the booming short-term rental market in the city. They decided to leverage their spare room by listing it on vacation rental platforms. Tourists and business travelers alike were drawn to the cozy space, providing the family with an additional source of income.

To further diversify their income, Mark and Lisa ventured into real estate. With careful research and planning, they invested in a small property, which they renovated and transformed into a profitable rental unit. The rental income became a stable and passive source of funds, helping them rebuild their financial foundation.

In the midst of their entrepreneurial endeavors, the Johnsons didn't neglect the power of education. Mark and Lisa attended workshops and online courses to enhance their skills, staying ahead in their respective fields. This continuous learning not only improved their expertise but also opened up new opportunities for income generation.

Over time, the Johnsons' commitment and strategic approach began to pay off. The combination of IT consulting, art sales, freelance work, short-term rentals, and real estate investments transformed their financial situation. They not only bounced back from bankruptcy but improved their quality of living in the vibrant and dynamic city that had presented them with challenges.

The Johnsons' success story became an inspiration in their community, demonstrating that resilience, collaboration, and diversification were key elements in overcoming financial hardships. As they celebrated their journey of triumph over adversity, Mark and Lisa enjoyed newfound stability they had created for themselves and their three children in the bustling heart of New York City.

Spencer's Story

In the city that never sleeps, Spencer, a determined 22-year-old college student, found himself caught in the whirlwind of bills and tuition fees, working a dead-end job that barely covered his basic expenses. Unwilling to succumb to the financial pressure, Spencer embarked on a journey of entrepreneurship that would change the trajectory of his life.

Spencer's first realization was that his skills in graphic design could be monetized. He started freelancing on various online platforms, offering his design services to clients around the world. As he built a reputation for delivering creative and high-quality work, his income from freelancing steadily increased, providing him with more financial stability.

Seeing the potential of e-commerce, Spencer decided to launch his own online store. Leveraging his design skills, he created a line of unique and trendy merchandise. From custom-designed T-shirts to accessories, his products gained popularity on social media platforms. With strategic marketing and a keen understanding of his target audience, Spencer's online store began generating a substantial income.

Recognizing the power of passive income, Spencer delved into affiliate marketing. He started a blog in his spare time, focusing on topics related to graphic design, entrepreneurship, and personal development. By incorporating affiliate links and sponsored content, Spencer turned his blog into a lucrative source of passive income.

To further diversify, Spencer explored the world of cryptocurrency. He educated himself about blockchain technology and started investing in different cryptocurrencies. As the value of his investments grew, Spencer found himself building a significant financial cushion.

With a keen interest in the stock market, Spencer decided to try his hand at day trading. He carefully studied market trends, developed a solid trading strategy, and began making profitable trades. His success in day trading added another dynamic stream of income to his growing portfolio.

In addition to his online ventures, Spencer recognized the demand for tutoring services on his college campus. Leveraging his expertise in graphic design and other subjects, he offered tutoring sessions to fellow students, charging a reasonable fee. This face-to-face interaction not only provided him with additional income but also helped him build a network within the academic community.

As Spencer approached his 25th birthday, he looked back on his journey with amazement. Through a combination of freelancing, e-commerce, affiliate marketing, cryptocurrency investments, day trading, and tutoring, he had transformed his financial situation. Spencer had not only managed to pay for his college expenses but had become a self-made millionaire before the age of 25.

Spencer's story became a testament to the possibilities that arise when one is willing to take risks, embrace entrepreneurship, and explore diverse income streams. As he continued to thrive in the dynamic landscape of online business and investments, Spencer became an inspiration for other college students, proving that age was no barrier to financial success with the right mindset and determination.

Annie Mae's Story

In the peaceful town of Savannah, Georgia, lived Annie Mae, a resilient 68-year-old widow facing the looming threat of losing her beloved home due to financial struggles. Determined to keep the roof over her head, Annie Mae embarked on a journey to create additional income streams and secure her cherished residence.

Annie Mae, despite her age, was known for her warm spirit and unwavering work ethic. She first tapped into her culinary skills, renowned in the community for her delicious homemade jams and preserves. Recognizing the demand for artisanal products, she began selling her preserves at local farmers' markets and community events. The unique flavors and quality of her preserves quickly garnered attention, creating a steady income stream.

Understanding the value of the local community, Annie Mae turned her attention to her neighborhood's gardening needs. With her green thumb, she started a small backyard garden, growing fresh produce. The surplus vegetables were sold to neighbors, and she even collaborated with a local grocery store to supply them with fresh, locally grown produce, providing another source of income.

Aware of the popularity of bed and breakfast accommodations in Savannah, Annie Mae decided to open her home to visitors. With its charming Southern hospitality and cozy atmosphere, her house became a sought-after destination for tourists. This venture not only generated income but also allowed Annie Mae to share her love for her community with visitors from near and far.

To maximize her limited resources, Annie Mae explored the gig economy. She offered her services as a local guide, providing personalized tours of Savannah's historic landmarks and hidden gems. This not only allowed her to share her passion for the town but also brought in extra income to support her financial goals.

In addition to her entrepreneurial efforts, Annie Mae took advantage of her wealth of life experiences. She began offering mentoring sessions to local entrepreneurs and individuals seeking guidance in life and business. This consultancy work not only showcased her wisdom but also added a consulting income stream to her growing repertoire.

As Annie Mae diversified her income streams, she also embraced the power of technology. With the help of a local tech-savvy volunteer, she set up an online platform to sell her preserves to a wider audience. This digital presence expanded her customer base beyond Savannah, allowing her to reach customers across the state and even beyond.

Through her unwavering determination and creativity, Annie Mae not only managed to create multiple streams of income but also saved her home from foreclosure. The combination of her homemade preserves, gardening, bed and breakfast, local guiding, and mentoring services transformed her financial situation, turning the tide just in time to secure the future of her cherished home in the heart of Savannah.

Annie Mae's story became an inspiration in the community, proving that resilience, resourcefulness, and a deep connection to one's passions and community could pave the way for financial success even in challenging circumstances. As Annie

Mae continued to thrive, she became a living testament to the enduring spirit of Savannah, where community and determination can triumph over adversity.

Fallon's Story

In the vibrant city of Austin, Texas, Fallon, a resilient 45-year-old woman, found herself facing an unexpected twist in her career journey as she lost her job. Undeterred by the setback, Fallon decided to turn adversity into opportunity and set out to create multiple streams of income to not only sustain herself but also to build a more secure financial future.

Fallon, with a background in marketing and a passion for writing, first explored the world of freelance content creation. She signed up on various online platforms, offering her services as a content writer and marketing consultant. Her expertise and creative flair quickly attracted clients, providing her with a steady income stream while allowing her the flexibility to work on her own terms.

Recognizing the rising demand for remote work solutions, Fallon decided to delve into the world of virtual assistance. Leveraging her organizational skills and attention to detail, she offered administrative and support services to entrepreneurs and small businesses. As her client base grew, so did her income, and she found herself managing tasks ranging from email management to social media coordination.

In addition to her freelance endeavors, Fallon identified an opportunity in the local community. Drawing inspiration from her love of fitness, she started offering outdoor fitness classes in a nearby park. The community embraced the idea, and soon, Fallon's fitness classes gained popularity. The classes not only provided her with an additional income source but also allowed her to combine her passion for wellness with entrepreneurial spirit.

To diversify further, Fallon explored the world of e-commerce. Drawing on her marketing background, she started an online store selling unique and curated products. The store gained traction through social media marketing, and Fallon's keen eye for trends contributed to its success. The e-commerce venture became another thriving stream of income.

Embracing the gig economy, Fallon also began offering her skills as a consultant in digital marketing and branding. Through online platforms, she connected with businesses looking to enhance their online presence. Her expertise in creating comprehensive marketing strategies became sought after, adding yet another dimension to her growing portfolio of income streams.

As Fallon navigated her newfound entrepreneurial journey, she continued to invest in her own education. She took online courses to stay updated on the latest trends in digital marketing, e-commerce, and virtual assistance. This ongoing learning not only enhanced her skills but also positioned her as a knowledgeable and reliable resource in her various ventures.

By the age of 48, Fallon looked back at her journey with pride. Through determination, adaptability, and a willingness to explore diverse income streams, she not only weathered the storm of job loss but created a more resilient financial foundation for herself. The combination of freelance writing, virtual assistance, fitness classes, e-commerce, and consulting transformed her life and outlook, proving that one can find success even in the face of unexpected challenges.

Fallon's story became an inspiration for others in Austin and beyond, highlighting the transformative power of resilience, creativity, and the pursuit of multiple income streams. As she continued to thrive in her diverse ventures, Fallon embraced the possibilities that arose from embracing change and turning setbacks into stepping stones toward a brighter and more fulfilling future.

Talented And Creative People

Talented and creative individuals often possess a combination of traits, experiences, and cognitive processes that contribute to their ability to excel in multiple areas. Here are some reasons why talented people may be creative in various domains:

Diverse Interests: Talented individuals tend to have diverse interests and curiosity about the world. They may explore different fields, leading to a broad range of experiences that can contribute to creativity.

Cross-Disciplinary Thinking: Creative individuals often engage in cross-disciplinary thinking, applying insights and approaches from one domain to another. This ability to connect seemingly unrelated ideas can lead to innovative solutions and creative outputs.

Adaptability: Talented individuals are often adaptable and open-minded. They may be more willing to step outside their comfort zones, try new things, and embrace challenges. This adaptability allows them to apply their skills in various contexts.

High Cognitive Abilities: Many talented individuals possess high cognitive abilities, such as critical thinking, problem-solving, and pattern recognition. These cognitive skills can be transferable across different domains, allowing them to excel in various areas.

Passion and Motivation: Passion can drive individuals to explore and excel in multiple areas. When someone is deeply passionate about a particular subject, they are more likely to invest time and effort, leading to a mastery of that domain.

Creativity as a Process: Creative individuals often view creativity as a process that can be applied across different fields. They may develop a mindset that values exploration, experimentation, and the generation of novel ideas, which can be applied universally.

Collaborative Nature: Many talented people are also collaborative and enjoy working with others. Collaborative efforts can lead to the exchange of ideas and perspectives, fostering creativity in various domains.

Continuous Learning: Talented individuals are often lifelong learners. They have a thirst for knowledge and are motivated to continuously acquire new skills. This constant learning can lead to a broad skill set and the ability to tackle diverse challenges.

High Levels of Energy and Drive: Talented and creative individuals often exhibit high levels of energy and drive. This motivation pushes them to pursue excellence in multiple areas and overcome obstacles in their creative endeavors.

Risk-Taking and Resilience: Creativity often involves taking risks and dealing with failures. Talented individuals may be more resilient in the face of setbacks, allowing them to learn from failures and apply those lessons to different pursuits.

Innovative Thinking: Talented individuals often possess a capacity for innovative thinking. They not only solve problems efficiently but also come up with new and unconventional solutions. This ability to think outside the box contributes to their creativity in multiple areas.

Pattern Recognition: Creative individuals tend to excel in recognizing patterns, whether they are visual, conceptual, or strategic. This skill allows them to make connections between seemingly disparate elements, leading to unique and creative insights.

Embracing Ambiguity: Creativity often thrives in environments with ambiguity. Talented individuals are comfortable navigating uncertainty and are more likely to embrace ambiguity, allowing them to explore uncharted territories and discover new possibilities.

Aesthetic Sensitivity: Many creative individuals have a heightened aesthetic sensitivity. This sensitivity extends beyond the traditional arts to encompass an appreciation for beauty, design, and elegance in various forms, fostering creativity across different domains.

Deep Focus and Flow: Talented people often experience a state of deep focus and flow when engaged in their work. This state of optimal experience allows them to immerse themselves fully in their creative endeavors, leading to enhanced productivity and innovative outcomes.

Strong Observational Skills: Creative individuals often have keen observational skills. They notice details, patterns, and nuances that others might overlook, allowing them to draw inspiration from their surroundings and incorporate unique elements into their work.

Effective Communication: Creativity is not just about generating ideas but also about effectively communicating them. Talented individuals often possess strong communication skills, enabling them to convey complex concepts in a way that resonates with others, fostering collaboration and shared creativity.

Intrinsic Motivation: While external recognition and rewards can be motivating, many creative individuals are driven by intrinsic motivation. They find joy and fulfillment in the process of creation itself, which sustains their enthusiasm and commitment across various endeavors.

Cognitive Flexibility: Cognitive flexibility is the ability to adapt thinking to different situations or tasks. Creative individuals tend to be cognitively flexible, easily shifting between different perspectives and problem-solving approaches, enhancing their versatility.

Personal Growth Mindset: Talented and creative individuals often have a growth mindset, believing that their abilities can be developed through dedication and hard work. This mindset encourages continuous improvement and resilience in the face of challenges.

In summary, the multifaceted nature of creativity in talented individuals arises from a combination of cognitive abilities, personality traits, mindset, and a rich tapestry of experiences. These factors interplay to create a fertile ground for innovation, allowing creative individuals to excel in various fields and pursuits throughout their lives.

Peace Of Mind

Having multiple streams of income can offer several psychological benefits compared to relying solely on a single source of income. Here are some key psychological advantages:

Reduced Financial Stress:
- *Security and Stability:* Diversifying your income sources provides a sense of financial security. Knowing that you have multiple streams can help mitigate the stress that comes with relying solely on one source, which may be subject to economic fluctuations or industry-specific challenges.

Increased Confidence and Empowerment:
- *Self-Reliance:* Diversification fosters a sense of self-reliance. You become less dependent on a single job or source of income, which can boost your confidence and empower you to take more calculated risks or pursue opportunities that align with your goals.

Flexibility and Adaptability:
- *Adaptation to Change:* Multiple income streams make you more adaptable to changes in the job market or industry. If one source is affected, you have others to fall back on, making it easier to weather economic downturns or unexpected life events.

Enhanced Work-Life Balance:

- *Reduced Overreliance on a Single Job:* Relying on one job may lead to overcommitment, longer working hours, and increased stress. Diversifying your income allows you to explore different work arrangements, potentially leading to a more balanced and fulfilling life.

Opportunities for Personal Growth:
- *Skill Development:* Managing multiple income streams often requires different skills and knowledge. This constant learning and adaptation can lead to personal and professional growth, fostering a mindset of continuous improvement.

Increased Financial Freedom:
- *Diversification for Financial Independence:* Having multiple streams of income can be a step towards financial independence. The psychological benefit lies in the sense of freedom and autonomy that comes with having the financial means to make choices aligned with your values and priorities.

Enhanced Long-Term Planning:
- *Financial Planning:* Diversification encourages individuals to engage in more robust financial planning. Knowing that income is not solely dependent on a single source enables better long-term financial strategizing, leading to a more secure future.

Mindset Shift:
- *Entrepreneurial Mindset:* Managing multiple income streams often requires an entrepreneurial mindset, even if you're not a traditional entrepreneur. This shift

in mindset can bring a sense of ownership and control over your financial destiny.

Parable Of The Talents

(Matthew 25:14-15):

In the Parable of the Talents, Jesus begins by describing a scenario where a man, representing the master or lord, is about to go on a journey. Before leaving, he entrusts his wealth to his servants, each according to their abilities. To one servant, he gives five talents; to another, two talents; and to the third, one talent. The distribution is based on the master's assessment of their individual capacities.

Responsibility and Initiative (Matthew 25:16-18):

The first two servants, who received five and two talents respectively, immediately set out to work with the resources given to them. They wisely invest and trade, doubling the talents entrusted to them. This reflects the importance of responsibility, initiative, and productive use of the gifts and opportunities bestowed by God. These servants demonstrate a proactive approach in utilizing their talents for growth and increase.

Fear and Inaction (Matthew 25:24-25):

The third servant, however, responds differently. Fearing the consequences of potential loss, he buries his one talent in the ground, opting for a safe but unproductive approach. This choice illustrates a lack of faith, initiative, and a failure to maximize the potential of the talent given to him. It highlights the detrimental impact of fear and the tendency to let opportunities pass by due to inaction.

Master's Return and Accountability (Matthew 25:19-30):

After a significant period, the master returns to settle accounts with his servants. The first two, who diligently invested their talents, present a double return to the master, and they receive commendation and reward. In contrast, the third servant, who hid his talent, faces the consequences of his inactivity. The master rebukes him for not at least investing the talent in a way that would yield some return. The master's response underscores the theme of accountability and the expectation of actively utilizing the gifts entrusted to us.

Principle of More Given to the Faithful (Matthew 25:29):

The master concludes the parable with a principle that resonates throughout Scripture: "For to everyone who has, more will be given, and he will have an abundance. But from him who does not have, even what he has will be taken away." This principle emphasizes the reward for faithful stewardship and the idea that God entrusts more to those who actively and responsibly use what they've been given, while those who neglect their responsibilities risk losing even the little they have.

Conclusion and Application (Matthew 25:30):

The parable concludes with the unfaithful servant being cast into outer darkness, where there is weeping and gnashing of teeth.

This harsh outcome underscores the seriousness of neglecting the talents and resources God provides. The parable serves as a call to action for believers, urging them to use their God-given abilities wisely, take risks for the sake of the Kingdom, and actively contribute to the growth of God's purposes on Earth. It teaches that faithfulness and diligence in stewardship lead to both earthly and eternal rewards, while negligence results in loss and judgment.

Lessons and Application for Believers:
The Parable of the Talents conveys several profound lessons for believers. Firstly, it emphasizes the diversity of God's gifts and the uniqueness of individual abilities. Each servant receives a different number of talents according to their capacity, suggesting that God has purposefully designed each person with distinctive skills and resources. This encourages believers to recognize and appreciate their own unique gifts and those of others.

The parable also stresses the importance of taking risks for the sake of God's Kingdom. The servants who invested their talents had to step out in faith, embracing the potential for both success and failure. This challenges believers to overcome fear, complacency, and the desire for comfort, prompting them to use their talents boldly and creatively in service to God and others.

Moreover, the master's response highlights God's desire for active and fruitful participation in His work. He commends those who multiplied their talents, indicating that God values and rewards faithful stewardship. This encourages believers to view their abilities not merely as personal assets but as resources to be invested for the greater good, contributing to the advancement of God's Kingdom on Earth.

The principle of "more given to the faithful" reinforces the idea that faithfulness in small things leads to increased responsibilities and blessings from God. This challenges believers to be diligent in their daily lives, recognizing that even seemingly insignificant actions can have a profound impact when done with a heart devoted to God.

In conclusion, the Parable of the Talents is a timeless and impactful teaching that calls believers to active and faithful stewardship of the gifts, opportunities, and resources entrusted to them by God. It challenges them to overcome fear, invest boldly in God's work, and anticipate both earthly and eternal rewards for their faithful service. The parable serves as a roadmap for living a purposeful and impactful Christian life, grounded in trust, responsibility, and active participation in God's redemptive plan.

A Call to Reflect and Evaluate:
The Parable of the Talents also invites believers to engage in regular self-reflection and evaluation. Each servant had to give an account of how they utilized the talents entrusted to them when the master returned. This aspect of the parable prompts believers to assess how they are using their time, abilities, and resources in their journey of faith.

It encourages a thoughtful examination of whether one is actively contributing to the growth of God's Kingdom or, out of fear or complacency, burying their talents. This reflective process becomes a spiritual discipline, fostering a deeper awareness of personal responsibility and accountability before God.

Grace and Second Chances:

While the parable highlights the consequences of unfaithfulness, it's essential to note the aspect of grace and second chances present in God's character. The unfaithful servant had the opportunity to invest his talent and make a positive impact, but he chose a path of inactivity. God's grace provides believers with opportunities for course correction and growth, emphasizing the importance of learning from past mistakes and actively engaging in fruitful stewardship.

This grace-filled dimension of the parable encourages believers to acknowledge and repent of any shortcomings in their stewardship, trusting in God's mercy and guidance to redirect their efforts toward faithful service.

Collaboration and Community Building:

While the parable focuses on individual stewardship, it also implies the potential for collaboration among believers. The servants who invested their talents might have worked together, shared insights, and contributed to a collective increase. This highlights the importance of community and mutual support within the body of believers, fostering an environment where talents are shared, multiplied, and used for the greater good.

Believers are encouraged not only to focus on personal growth but also to actively participate in building a community that values and encourages the development of each member's unique talents. The parable, therefore, speaks to the interconnectedness of believers in their journey of faith.

The Parable of the Talents continues to resonate as a rich source of wisdom and guidance for believers, calling them to reflection, active participation, and collaborative efforts in advancing God's Kingdom. It encompasses themes of responsibility, accountability, grace, and the transformative power of faithful stewardship within the context of a supportive community of believers.

One of the unexpected benefits of this transformative journey was the discovery of untapped potential within myself. Unleashing my creativity and entrepreneurial spirit allowed me to explore facets of my talents that had previously remained dormant. It was a revelation that went beyond monetary gains, providing a deep sense of self-discovery and personal growth.

The diversified income streams provided a safety net during economic uncertainties, demonstrating the resilience of a well-structured portfolio. No longer reliant on a single source of income, I felt liberated from the constraints of traditional employment and embraced the freedom to shape my schedule and pursue projects aligned with my values.

Moreover, the newfound financial stability enabled me to invest in further personal and professional development. I could allocate resources to expand my skill set, explore new interests, and contribute to causes that held personal significance. This holistic approach to life not only enhanced my capabilities but also fostered a sense of balance and well-being.

As the momentum of my entrepreneurial journey continued, I began to inspire others to embark on their paths of self-discovery and income diversification. Becoming a mentor and sharing my experiences became an integral part of my mission, as I recognized the transformative potential within everyone to create a life that harmonizes with their passions.

In retrospect, changing my life forever by leveraging my gifts and talents to create multiple streams of income was not just a financial triumph but a holistic metamorphosis. It reshaped my identity, instilled a sense of purpose, and illuminated the boundless possibilities that arise when one aligns their livelihood with their truest self. This journey was a testament to the transformative power of embracing one's unique abilities and channeling them into avenues that not only sustain but enrich every facet of life.

You Can Do It

Embarking on a journey to change your life by leveraging your gifts and talents to create multiple streams of income involves a deliberate and strategic approach. Begin by engaging in deep self-reflection to identify your unique skills, passions, and interests. Recognize that these attributes are not just hobbies but potential sources of income.

Invest time in continuous learning and skill development. Acquire certifications, attend workshops, and seek mentorship to enhance your capabilities. This commitment to improvement not only sharpens your skills but also positions you as an expert in your chosen field.

Establish a strong online presence to showcase your talents and reach a broader audience. Create a professional website or portfolio, and leverage social media platforms to connect with potential clients and collaborators. The digital landscape provides an invaluable platform to market your skills and attract opportunities.

Diversify your income streams by exploring various avenues related to your passions. This could include freelancing, consulting, creating and selling products, or offering online courses. Each income stream adds a layer of stability and resilience to your overall financial strategy.

Networking is a critical component of this journey. Engage with like-minded individuals, attend industry events, and participate in online communities to expand your network. Building meaningful connections can lead to collaborations, partnerships, and opportunities that further enhance your entrepreneurial pursuits.

Embrace an entrepreneurial mindset. Approach challenges as opportunities for growth, maintain a strong work ethic, and remain adaptable to changes in the business landscape. This mindset shift empowers you to navigate setbacks with resilience and fosters a proactive approach to achieving your goals.

As you build momentum in your journey, consider reinvesting in yourself. Allocate resources to personal and professional development, exploring new skills and interests. The ability to adapt and evolve will be crucial in sustaining long-term success.

1. Self-Assessment:

- Identify your passions and talents: Make a list of activities and skills you genuinely enjoy and excel at.
- Evaluate your strengths and weaknesses: Assess the skills you possess and areas where you can improve.

2. Set Clear Goals:

- Define your long-term goals: Identify where you want to be in the next 1, 3, and 5 years.
- Break down goals into smaller milestones: Create achievable short-term objectives to keep yourself motivated.

3. Skill Development:

- Invest in training and education: Identify the skills needed to monetize your talents and pursue relevant courses or workshops.
- Leverage online platforms: Use platforms like Coursera, Udemy, or Skillshare for affordable and accessible learning opportunities.

4. Build a Portfolio:

- Showcase your talents: Create an online portfolio highlighting your skills, projects, and achievements.
- Collect testimonials: Request recommendations from colleagues, mentors, or clients to add credibility.

5. Network and Mentorship:

- Attend industry events: Connect with professionals in your field, attend workshops, and join relevant online communities.
- Seek mentorship: Find a mentor who has successfully transitioned from a traditional job to a talent-based career.

6. Side Projects:

- Start small: Begin working on passion projects in your free time to gain experience and build a portfolio.
- Test the market: Validate your talents by offering small services or products to friends, family, or online communities.

7. Financial Planning:

- Create a budget: Assess your current financial situation and develop a budget to sustain yourself during the transition.
- Save for emergencies: Set aside a financial safety net to cover unexpected expenses.

8. Freelancing or Part-Time Work:

- Ease into the transition: Consider taking on freelance projects or part-time work related to your talents while still at your job.
- Build a client base: Use freelance opportunities to establish a network and gain experience.

9. Marketing and Branding:

- Create a personal brand: Develop a unique identity that represents your talents and sets you apart from others.
- Utilize social media: Leverage platforms like LinkedIn, Instagram, or Twitter to showcase your work and connect with potential clients.

10. Evaluate and Adjust:

- Regularly assess your progress: Review your goals, achievements, and challenges to adjust your strategy as needed.
- Be flexible: Adapt to changes in the market, industry trends, or personal circumstances.

Remember that the transition may take time, and there will be challenges along the way. Stay persistent, remain adaptable, and continue refining your talents to create a sustainable and fulfilling career.

I'm so proud of you for reading this book and making an effort to change your life forever. God gives us all talents and purpose. Be careful not squander yours,

Here is a poem that explains perfectly the journey of those who are willing to step out on faith and take a chance to change their life forever. Utilizing your gifts and talents and believing in yourself takes courage and determination. It is not for the faint of heart. You have to remind yourself daily that you are worth it.

Poem

In a world of choices vast and wide,

Where dreams and hopes do coincide,

A lesson echoes through the air,
Never put all your eggs in one rare.

Baskets woven with threads of chance,

Hold futures, each a unique dance.

Diversify, the wise ones say,

Spread your hopes in a vast array.

For in the garden of life's design,

Variety paints a path divine.

One basket may sway with the wind,

While others sturdy, resilience pinned.

In ventures bold and dreams so grand,

Avoid the grip of a single strand.

For when the unexpected storm does rise,

Distributed strength, the key to prize.

Imagine a farmer with fields untold,

A bounty of stories waiting to be told.

Corn and wheat, and apples in a tree,

Each a chapter in life's library.

In the market of chances, diverse and wide,

Let not your destiny be simplified.

In every venture, a basket to hold,

A tapestry of tales, both young and old.

So, heed this counsel, wise and true,

In life's grand tapestry, a lesson to view.

Spread your dreams, let them hatch and grow,

In various baskets, let your potential flow.

For when the winds of change do blow,

And uncertainty casts its shadow,

Your eggs, well-placed, in baskets arrayed,

Ensure that no dream will be betrayed.

Ruff-Moore, Kim. *Never Put All Your Eggs In One Basket*. Ruff Moore Publishing, 2024.

Sources cited within the book:

Warren Buffet Wiki: https://en.wikipedia.org/wiki/Warren_Buffett
Magic Earvin Johnson Wiki: https://en.wikipedia.org/wiki/Magic_Johnson
Mary Kay Ash Wiki: https://en.wikipedia.org/wiki/Mary_Kay_Ash
Sheila Johnson Wiki: https://en.wikipedia.org/wiki/Sheila_Johnson
Cathy Hughes Wiki: https://en.wikipedia.org/wiki/Cathy_Hughes
Investopedia: https://www.investopedia.com/
Parable of Talents, King James Bible Edition 23
Bible Scriptures - Various passages from the Bible
- Bible Hub: https://biblehub.com/

Meet Kim Ruff Moore: Beloved Author, Storyteller, and Literacy Advocate

Kim Ruff Moore is a prolific author with over 90 books, writing heartfelt children's stories and impactful Christian self-help titles. As the founder of the Please Read Project, Kim is dedicated to promoting literacy, donating her books to children and adults who need them most. Her diverse catalog of children's books, including favorites like the *Pebo Pig Prefers* and *Suzzie Mocha* series, brings joy and imagination to readers of all ages. Among her inspiring adult works are *I Still Have Joy*, *Never Put All Your Eggs in One Basket*, *Waymaker*, and *Girl Mash the Gas*.

Kim's books are widely available at Walmart, Barnes & Noble, Books-A-Million, Harvard Book Store, and other major retailers. Beyond writing, she's a Stellar Award-winning singer-songwriter and a member of The New Consolers with her husband, Jeffery Moore.

Discover more about Kim's work at kimruffmoore.com and ruffmooremedia.com.